SIMPLE TRUTHS

LOST & FOUND - BOOK ONE

MICHELLE DALTON

A CMIANA PUBLISHERS

To my Hubster and the Penguins of Simons Town.

GLOSSARY

Ag Tog: A polite South African term expressing sympathy, distress or surprise. (Ah-gh T-oh-gh)

Amakhosi: The big chief in charge. It is a combination of Zulu and Xhosa. (Ah-mah-koh-sie)

AWOL: Absent Without Leave.

Aikona: No. (Eye-koh-nah)

Babalas: A hangover. (Ba-ba-lah-s)

Bakkie: A UTE or pickup truck. (Bah-kie)

Bliksem: Means lightning in Afrikaans but is also used as a curse. (Blu-k-sim)

Blerrie: South Africanism for Bloody the British informal offensive to express annoyance.

Boet: Short for boetie, (boot/booty) meaning brother.

Bras: South African colloquial term for bro/buddy/brother in arms.

Chooki: Jail or prison. (Chew-kie)

Crim: South African slang for criminal.

Dagga: Pronounced by grinding the 'g' daghagha – Marijuana. (Dah-Gha . . . grate the 'g' sound)

Dof: Dim, slow. (Doh-f)

Eish: An informal South African exclamation to express a range of emotions from surprise, annoyance, and exasperation. (Eee-sh)

ED: Emergency Department.

Fliek: Movie. (Fli-k)

Fynbos: Indigenous bushland in the cape. (F-ai-n-b-oh-s)

Gat gabbas: A derogatory term for gay. (Grate the 'g' sound. Gah-t Gah-bas)

Gautenger: A person from the province of Gauteng South Africa.

Gham: A derogatory term used to degrade a person of color.

Groot Kop: The person in charge. Head honcho, or inflated ego. (Grate the 'g' sound. G-rrr-oh-t K-oh-p)

Hayibo: South African slang interjection indicating disbelief, moral disgust, surprise. (Hi – i – boh)

Hottentot: A racial term used to describe the Khoisan but used as a derogatory term to degrade people. (Hoh-ten-toh-t)

Howzit: South African slang for hello. (How-z-it)

Ja/Nee: Yes/no in English. A South Africanism used to signal agreement, hesitation, or used when a person tries to solicit a comment. (Y-ah N-ea 'r')

Kak: South African 'Taboo' word for manure. (K-ah-k)

Lekka: A South Africanism meaning nice, good, enjoyable, stunning, awesome. (Leh-k-er)

Nunu: Zulu – meaning baby. A term of endearment. (Nooh-nooh)

Nooit: Never. (N-oi-t)

Ole Toppie: Old Man

Oom: Uncle. (oowem)

Ouma: Grandmother. (Oh-mah)

Oupa: Grandfather. (Oh-pah)

Pissy: A South Africanism for a scaredy-cat or chicken.

Poophol: Arsehole. (pooh-p-hol)

Rand: South African currency.

Riempies: Strips of rawhide. (Reem-peas)

Roemertopf: A clay cook pot. (Rom-er-tof)

Sangoma: A traditional healer or diviner.

Shebeen: Irish, Scottish and South African term for an unlicensed tavern or drinking hole.

Sjambok: A whip (sham – boh – k)

Sjoe: South Africa. an exclamation expressive of surprise, admiration, exhaustion, etc. (Shoe)

Skebenga: A criminal. (Skha-ben-gah)

Skelm: A con artist. Secretive. (S-khel-m)

Slaap: Sleep. (Sl-ah-p)

Stoep: Verandah or porch. (Stoop)

Special-special: A colloquial South African term expressing value or endearment.

Spooky: A pet name meaning little ghost or shadow. (Sp-hoh-kie)

Suikerbos: A shrub indigenous to the cape—Sugar Bush. (S-oi-k-errr-b-oh-s)

Tjommies: Buddies. (choh-mies)

To Pitch: A South Africanism meaning to arrive or visit.

Tsotsi: A criminal. (Ts-haw -t-sy)

"Geseende Vader. Ons Dank U vir die voorreg wat hier voor ons op die tafel…" Blessed Father. We thank you for the blessings laid out before us on this table.

Umfazi: Woman. (Ohm-fah-zie)

Veldt: Bush. (felt)

Voertsek: Buzz off. (Foot-sack)

Yebo: Zulu for Yes. (yeah-boh)

PROLOGUE

THE CLINIC AT THE FAR NORTH END OF THE KOINADUGU District in Sierra Leone is busy, sticky, zooms with flies, and reeks of death. Another outbreak of Cholera in the small, poverty-stricken village has all the staff of our deployment of Doctors Without Borders at their wits end.

The canvas walls of the tent billow as hot wind slaps them to and fro, bringing little relief but only adding to the misery of life. My guide and self-proclaimed protector, Max, holds back the flap of the door for me to step out and stand beneath a thread-bare tarp tied between two dead stumps. It provides little relief as a makeshift shield from the sun. In the distance, a herd of goats bleat when a lone bull dares to drink from the same trough that they do. The shade, distributed to them by trees I've never bothered to learn about, is sparse and practically nonexistent; here leaves, like people, wither as soon as they bloom.

"Dokta!" a rickety, parched voice calls out.

I look to my left as I duck and step out into the scorching African morning.

A woman, small in stature but strong in presence, walks toward me. Her grey hair is plaited in a way that pulls the skin of her face in tight lines around her eyes. Around her neck, wrists, and ankles hang leather straps decorated with feathers, stones, and beads. Her tan-colored three quarter pants and blue button-up top are well worn, but clean. Over her shoulder hangs a handmade leather bag decorated in beads and more: small bones. A bag I know from experience holds specially engraved bones, teeth, and other paraphernalia used by her kind.

"Be gon wit ya, woman!"

Max the ever loyal, steps forward and puts himself between the woman and me.

I tuck a wayward strand of my thick blond mop behind my ear. "It's okay. She means no harm." I place a hand on his shoulder.

"Aye, she be da devil with dem eyes."

"Shh, Max," I plead. "How can I help?" I ask, trying not to focus on her gaze. Her eyes, one blue as the sky crowning our heads and the other as brown as the darkest chocolate ever tempered are the mark of a witch, according to local lore.

I lower my gaze respectfully.

"I no be meanin ta bother." Her voice softens in a respectful tone as she apologizes and confirms my instincts.

Her skin is as leathery as her voice, but her body is strong. Her arms and legs, though slim, are lithe and toned, and her general appearance has no tell of the illness currently running rife through the village.

"Are you ill?" My hand instinctively rubs my tummy as I'm not sure why else she'd be here.

The woman throws her head back, and a cackle cracks like a whip through the heat-drenched air. Her laughter ceases as suddenly as it begins, and the woman inches closer.

Max tries to stand between us, but I shake my head as she reaches out and pinches my chin between her forefinger and thumb. She smells of smoldering fire and tobacco as she pins me to the spot with her mismatched gaze. For a moment, I am lost in the swirl of blue and brown.

"Noh, Dokta. I be free from da bad juju of dis place. But tis yew I cum ta see."

Her words carry no threat of harm or dreaded curses - not that I believe in curses - but the look in those eyes almost bring me to my knees.

1

I DO NOT BELIEVE IN PROPHECIES, CURSES, OR DREAMS!

The words are on repeat in my brain as I make my way off the plane at Cape Town International. The long, bumpy flight from Sierra Leone has left me exhausted, and prone to doubt and silly, soppy emotions. It's well after ten p.m, but the sun never sets before eleven in the summer; for that I am grateful.

My sudden resignation from my job has nothing to do with some warning from an old lady with heterochromia.

Her words plagued me for days after she'd delivered her prophecy.

"There be a time for all tha things in dis world, and now be yours. For da sun and da moon, they sing a song of reegret, shan't you heed their words. Hasten home for it be time for your heart ta show da way. Hasten home or you will com ta greef and neva forgive your heart. Them bad

shadows, they are collecting, sourin' da graypes of your roots. Hasten home, waste no time, for there beneet tha twisted arms of weesdom waits peace, waits trust, waits harmony and your foreva lov."

Dark shadows? Perhaps her words *were* a curse. They'd haunted me in my dreams most of all—torrid night terrors with blood soaking the soil of Pa's vineyard. The farmhouse devoured by large angry flames. Hordes of malicious humans converging on the farm, chanting curses and illegally claiming what was not theirs.

And then they'd fade, the shadows melting into the light as a hand reached out to take mine. The face of the boy who'd stolen my heart all those years ago would appear. His arms wrapped around my body . . .

Only my messed-up subconscious could serve up both a nightmare and an erotic dream in a single night's sleep.

I'd woken drenched in sweat, with the memory of Thomas's touch lingering on my skin and his taste on my lips. It left me panting and filled with longing for him. Him, with those delicious brown eyes—my first kiss, and my only love, frozen in my heart forever.

I've not thought of him in a long, long time. So why now? Oh yes, I forgot: some random words spoken in some godforsaken village in North Africa.

My cheeks burn as I relive the steamy memories: his hands gliding up the inside of my legs and the touch of his lips on my neck. My nipples instantly react to the memory of the dream as they push against the light fabric of my cotton top.

It was all so real—too real. I glance around, afraid some passerby can read my naughty thoughts. But everyone is on their own mission to get home, and no one pays much attention to the world about them.

Ugh, I'm pathetic.

I've spent the last week trying to convince myself I am not returning home because of him, but because I missed my pa. I'd been gone from home long enough, and Koinadugu District and Doctors Without Borders had seen enough of me.

I chuck my bag into the boot of my rental and climb into the driver's seat. The airport is crawling with travelers, coming and going, some appearing excited and others apprehensive.

I rest my head on the seat and take a deep breath.

Nobody knows I'm here. I want to surprise Pa, *and* I need to know he is safe.

I open my eyes and start the engine. Slowly I guide the small hatchback out of the parking lot, then slip onto the exit road, then cautiously navigate the lanes and ignore the irritated, hooting traffic. At last, I come to the main road.

Tall buildings begin to sprout the closer I get to the city. The traffic has shifted from irritated to cutthroat. Hooligans with cars zigzag in and out of fast-moving lanes whilst honking their horns and shouting profanities at anyone in their way. Taxis pull to a dead stop in the middle of it all to off-load or collect passengers. Their vehicles are packed beyond capacity; I swear I can see the doors bulge.

I almost prefer the rickety roads of Kabala to this.

I lean back into the scratchy fabric-covered seat of my rental and grip the wheel a little tighter as I patiently make my way toward the off-ramp and on to the highway which will lead to our family vineyard in Constantia. I glance at the console clock—I should be there in around forty-five minutes.

A million feelings and thoughts pummel my exhausted mind as I drive through areas and past icons I haven't seen in more than a decade.

It's an unusually still day. A thick cloud of mist has draped itself neatly over our flat-topped icon, Table Mountain, like a dusk-tainted tablecloth. The Cape has changed; it's busier and dirtier than I remember.

The sidewalks are littered with takeaway cups and bags, not unlike any other city in South Africa or Africa for that matter.

The poor beg at every traffic light, and make sure to remain vigilant for any *tsotsis* on the prowl. It's not Johannesburg, where hijacking is part of everyday life, but I'm still cautious; criminals are everywhere.

But it's still my home and it's so good to be back.

A police van races past me as I turn on to the highway.

Is my brother, Raymond out? Has he returned home? Is he the danger? I hope not.

My nerves zing and excitement buzzes around my insides. I flick on the radio and a local news station drizzles out from the speakers. The woman's voice is young and monotonous.

"An unmarked trawler has run aground in the early hours of this morning off the shores of Saldanha Bay. While the captain was missing, the crew were found onboard, and at least twenty children, ranging from the ages of sixteen down to four years old, were discovered below deck in poor health."

I flick to another station and the familiar tune of a local South African artist calms my rattled insides. I love Prime Circle.

I take note of the signboards overhead and turn on my indicator when I see my exit coming up.

I can't wait to see Pa.

The cityscape dies away and soon I am surrounded by familiar lush green surroundings. Vineyards blanket the hills and valleys. Tall trees and distant highlands paint a sublime vista that is dotted with beautiful calla lilies growing wild in the untouched patches along the side of the road.

I spot the entrance, flick on my indicator, and turn the tiny sedan onto the drive leading up to our wine farm.

It's the beginning of summer so the sun will set close to midnight. Its golden fingers strike the bronze letters bolted to the white wall, now creating a bright halo which causes me to squint.

Nooitgedacht.

The name given to this farm over two hundred years ago.

Black iron gates stand open and inviting. The oak trees have grown. Their gnarled arms stretch out across the path, reaching for one another, and form a dark green canopy above me. It's hard to pretend I've not been gone a decade.

I push on the button and my window slides down. The sharp scents of grape, damp soil, and the familiar invade my lungs.

I am home.

Unlike other farm-owners, Pa has kept his winery small and manageable. There's no restaurant for tourists. Only a small new-brick building to the far side where, according to our Skype sessions, he allows the odd tour bus to stop by for a tasting. He reckons by keeping the tourists at bay, he adds to the allurement of his famous brand.

I slip the car into the neatly graveled, horse-shoe drive which curves past the front door of the Cape-Dutch-style house. This distinctive Western Cape architectural home, with its ornate rounded gables and large wooden sash cottage-windowed façade, greets me with a front door standing wide open. I hope it's because Grace is inside. It's never safe to leave a door open or unlocked, especially not on a farm.

Nevertheless, I allow my eyes to drink in the beauty of this stoic old building.

The thatch is new and neat. The black tar it's been treated with is in stark contrast to the whitewashed H-shaped house flanked by two wings running perpendicular to it.

This is the place of my birth, the house I grew up in, the same home which has brought me much joy, loss, and a broken heart, and comforted me in my darkest hour. I can still hear Ma calling me in from the vineyards for dinner, and Pa's deep-bellied laughter. A magical place with the sun sinking behind the distant hills as a boy and a girl shared a stolen kiss and some wine . . . I shake my head and push away that memory.

I get out of the car, stretching my hands above my head as I look this way and that. Few things have changed here. Though it's quieter and the smell of Ma's cooking no longer hovers as an open invitation at the front door, it is where I belong. I trot up the steps and stop.

"Spooky?"

His pet name for me, which stuck once I turned three and formed a habit of following him everywhere, washes away the knot of ice sitting in my belly. I turn to find my father making his way toward the house from the cellar, where all the barrels of wine are stored to age. He is greyer and rounder, but his sky-blue gaze is as bright as ever.

"Pa!" I run down the steps and wrap myself around his portly body.

His arms wind vise-like around me, and a damp

warmth soaks my shoulder. "You're back?" He lets go, leans back, and grips both hands on my shoulders. His puzzled eyes swim in relief and happiness.

"Yes."

"For a visit?"

"No, Pa. For good."

"What's wrong?" His gaze travels over my face.

"Nothing. It was just time to come home." I pat his arm and we make our way inside.

We pass the formal lounge, and an echo from an unwanted memory runs its ice-cold fingers from the tip of my toes, up my spine, and grips me at the base of my skull. There, in Ma's show cabinet, stands the silver cup. An heirloom passed down from Pa's French Huguenot ancestors. The very same cup I stole from its encased prison one night over a decade ago, to share a stolen sip of wine with a boy I'd given both my heart and my first kiss to.

I ignore its pull. It holds too many painful memories. Memories I've spent half a lifetime trying to forget.

There be a time for all tha things in dis world, and now be yours. For da sun and da moon they sing a song of reegret, shan't you heed their words. Hasten home, for it be time for your heart ta show da way . . .

2

LIEUTENANT THOMAS CAMPBELL LEANED AGAINST THE ancient fig tree, with its thick, gnarled branches stretching out over the waterfront and lawn where picnickers laughed and enjoyed the beauty surrounding them. His favorite spot in Simon's Town spread itself out across the harbor in an emerald blanket of summer and pleasure. It must be a good day for sailing and fishing; there were barely any boats docked at their jetties today.

The area had been built up and revamped over the last few years. A fancy hotel stood off to one side, all its rooms gazing out over the water. Small boutiques and curio shops had sprouted along the road opposite the quay, while tourists and holidaymakers decorated the paths and cafes like baubles on a Christmas tree.

But the ancient fig tree had been left in peace to push its twisted fat roots deeper into the sandy soil. It reminded him of a wise old man, one who stood and watched over the comings and goings of all who lived there. It whispered tales to him as the wind danced through its large, dark green leaves. His favorite, and one which it had repeated often, was that of two lovers reuniting. Agh, but it was all cobwebs and birds' nests. Love was a dream and not meant for him anyway.

Thomas placed the dark blue baseball cap, which matched his uniform, on the bench beside him and sat. He rubbed his short, titian cropped hair with the heel of his hand. It was a hot day, and the uniform's heavy material didn't help.

He rarely spent his lunch hour in the noisy mess with the other Navy personnel. Here beneath the twisted outstretched limbs of his ancient friend he found solace. He wasn't religious. His Uncle Ibrahim's beatings and staunch denunciation of him as a '*kaffir*' put him off early in his life. It still haunted him. Though he did like to believe there was a greater being out there somewhere.

Every person needed to come to terms with their lives, and the one way to do that was to find peace and have faith. Besides love, it was what gave meaning to life. He had no one to love, not in the way of a caring family or a lover, but he had this.

He switched his phone to silent, noticing another message from his uncle. Why, after all this time, was Ibrahim trying to make contact? With the tap of his thumb he deleted it and peeled open the container of pasta, he'd purchased at the local deli, and ate.

He was tired, more so than usual. It was the dreams. He hadn't had them in years. Dreams which he refused to think on now for fear his body might react the way it had when he'd awoken: hard, excited, and hungry. It wasn't simply the physicality of the dreams which had toppled his peaceful rest, but also his heart. The hurt and loss from a long time ago had resurfaced and, even now, scorched the fractured center of his soul.

Why now? Why her?

With the questions still fresh in his mind, Thomas looked up and froze, fork midair. The food-filled utensil dropped in the dish as he placed it on the bench beside him. He rubbed his eyes. This couldn't be. After all these years?

Making her way toward the ice crème vendor, a few meters from where Thomas sat, was a blonde vision. Her hair, infused with strands of candy pink and baby blue, like candied faerie floss, was bundled atop her head, evidence of her hectic day.

He watched as the woman dressed in stained, green hospital scrubs closed her eyes—from memory they were cyan like tropical waters—and licked her frozen delicacy.

Rochelle Le Roux?

Could it be?

Last he'd heard, she'd moved to England to study medicine. That was a long time ago.

Memories of that night fourteen years in the past rushed at him like a raging water buffalo. Because of his uncle's political connections, they'd attended a gathering of the local wine farmers. Ibrahim had persuaded Derrek to host the evening.

The event happened to fall on her sixteenth birthday.

Derrek Le Roux and his Uncle Ibrahim Abad were at the center of historical land negotiations between the farmers, the Cape Malay community, the Bantu people, and the Khoisan. There was a need for redistribution of land. But as far as Thomas could figure out, there were those who simply wanted something for nothing, such as Ibrahim and his ilk, and those who saw the danger in not traversing the situation with care and respect.

They'd had the best of intentions—or at least Derrek Le Roux and the Khoisan chief had. But the dealings quickly turned to ash and dust as treachery by the Bantu chief and Ibrahim, both refused to acknowledge the Khoi Khoi's heritage rights, soon became evident. Back then, Thomas had not cared. His attention had been utterly monopolized by the girl standing sulking in the corner.

His attraction to Rochelle . . . and hers to him . . . was immediate; the results - prolific and embarrassing. His mind drifted a little further to her shy smiles and luminescent gaze. Hands entwined, they'd tiptoed along the halls and borrowed a cup from a glass cabinet; its sentimental value had not been lost on his sixteen-year-old self. She'd grabbed a bottle of wine from the rack and together they had wandered out to the vineyards.

Their fateful decision to share the zesty red ambrosia, and a single kiss beneath the stars, had ended in heartbreak and tears.

After all, he was considered a half-breed of a differing faith, and she, a white Afrikaans girl. The daughter of one of the most affluent wine farmers in the district. But he knew beyond a doubt what they had shared was real, and more valuable than the conflicting beliefs of two cultures.

The memory of the strange sensation he'd experienced as their lips had touched returned, and still had the power to flip his insides over.

He'd seen her only once after that. The day she'd waited for him outside his school gates. But never again. His heart had bled when he'd had to turn his back on her. Every fiber of his being had wanted to walk up to her and wrap his arms around her, but he was forbidden to make contact, threatened with another severe beating if he ever spoke to her again. His uncle had made a point to accompany him to prayers every day after that. Determined to wash away his half-bred bastard sins with contemplation and devotion. He was kept under lock and key until the day he turned eighteen. No more embarrassment from the child born of shame—the orphan, the outcast.

Thomas watched Rochelle finish her ice crème. He would never forget her lingering gaze. It'd haunted his dreams for years, along with her plump cherry-red lips, milk-white skin, and a laugh which he could only equate to that of an angel's. She hadn't grown much in height, but other areas . . . Even in her scrubs, one couldn't miss the voluptuous curves. Her bone structure was fine and sharp.

Thomas jumped up from where he sat. It was fate, her being here. Now was his chance!

But memories of that night so long ago . . . the anger in his uncle's eyes, the sordid whispers of the guests as he was dragged away, her heartbreak as he turned his back on her outside the school gates . . . squashed his exuberance.

His cell phone vibrated. An urgent meeting was being called by the rear admiral at headquarters. Too shocked to wonder why he was being summoned, Thomas threw the remainder of his lunch in the bin and gave Rochelle one last glance.

Perhaps it was best to leave her where she belonged—in the past with all the other boyhood scars.

———

IT'S BEEN a busy month since I left Sierra Leone, but I've made a point of seeing Pa every week.

Nothing has changed in the ten years I've been gone. I left right after high school graduation to study medicine at Oxford and got offered the job with Doctors Without Borders not long after I completed my residency. Pa has kept the house exactly as Ma left it.

I stop at the oval oak table in the entrance. On it sits a family photo. *I miss her.* The anger of the pain she'd endured, the slow tormented death she'd been handed, twists in my gut. That was the day I turned my back on faith and any belief that there was a benevolent anything somewhere out there.

Ma passed eleven years ago. Breast cancer. It almost killed Pa too. Theirs was a once-in-a-lifetime love. A connection I'd once thought to have for myself.

An unbidden memory rushes to the forefront of my mind. The soft touch of Thomas' lips on mine . . . My heart skips a beat. Fourteen years is forever, but not forever enough to soothe a fractured heart. But that was then. I was young and naïve. Though I'd been told that time would heal, it has done nothing of the sort.

I've ignored the urge to look him up on the internet. He's probably long gone by now. Married with kids and a career of his own.

I slip off my sandals at the entrance to the kitchen, so I can enjoy the cool of the polished concrete floor as it soothes my tired soles.

"Hi, Pa." I lean down and kiss his cheek. Already seated at the kitchen table, he twirls a wine glass in one hand as his other grips the *Daily News*.

"Hello, Spook."

"What's that on the front page?" I ask as I scan the bold headline.

"Agh, bad business this . . ." He puts down his glass and waves toward the page. "Children being ripped from the back seats of their parents' cars in hijackings, and teenagers going missing. The police seem to think there's a ring of human traffickers roaming the Cape for easy pickings. They're linking it to those poor little souls found on that ship which ran aground in Saldanha."

Pa's right; it is a bad business. I thought I'd left a lot of ugly back in Sierra Leone, but ugly, it seems, is to be found in every corner of this world.

"*Ja.* The cops brought in a handful of them over the weekend. I heard one of the constables say that the coast guard managed to stop a second boat. They're using fishing trawlers to carry them off to goodness knows where." I shake away the memory of small sad eyes which had looked to me for safety as I inspected a tiny bruised body for injuries children her age should never experience. Hell, not even adults should.

"Agh no, Spook. You had to treat the poor little things?" His gaze narrows as he inspects my face.

"It's okay, Pa. We managed. It was heartbreaking though," I say.

"Another boat, eh? I was hoping the last one would have deterred the bastards." Pa slaps a hand on the paper laying innocently on the table.

I shrug and pour myself some of the zesty red standing open on the table. Its aroma stirs something hidden deep within me. I put it down to the resurfacing nostalgia at being home.

"Been busy?" Pa asks, sipping his wine.

"I love my new apartment and the fact it's got hot running water. Oh, the things we take for granted." I sip my wine, and Pa chuckles.

Stars, smiles, and hungry lips on mine flash across my mind. A wave of fire runs up from my shoulders, burning my neck, and invades my cheeks with its glowering embarrassment. I hold the glass away from me and frown at Pa, who's wearing an expression of complete innocence. I bring the glass back to my nose, then sip. "Is this the same wine as . . .?"

"As?" he asks, feigning ignorance.

I decide not to take the bait and shake my head. "There is no room for love in my life, Pa."

"You mean fear has filled that part of your heart and left you in the dark?" Pa lifts his glass and taps the edge against mine where it stands on the table. The sharp *ting* of crystal against crystal reverberates through me. Pa is determined. I lean back and consider the glass.

Seconds of silence fall like soft rain before the old man sighs and leans forward. "*Ja, nee* my girl. We only miss them when they're no longer ours . . . or with us." His eyes darken a little.

His words carry great meaning. He misses Mom. Like me, he has his own regrets to work through and make peace with.

The air grows dank with dark memories and broken hearts.

Time to change the subject.

I stand and make my way over to the warming tray on the kitchen counter behind me. "Smells divine." I lift the lid of the *roemertopf*. Ma loved her clay cooking pots and Pa has looked after them so well.

Grace, my father's housekeeper and cook phenomena, has conjured an apricot chicken like no other. My stomach rumbles in excitement.

"How's your week been? You enjoying the boring hours of hospital work?" A mischievous grin sneaks across Pa's face as he refills his glass.

"Actually, it's great. The emergency department is a never-ending source of excitement and, best of all, there's actual medicine available with which to treat our patients. No red tape or hoop jumping and bribery. Just pure, simple medicine." I don't mention the druggie who burst in the other night swinging the business end of a broken bottle at us while demanding his fix. Thank goodness for hospital security.

"Ja, well it's all sunshine and roses in the private sector. Bet you'd find the same problems in the government hospitals though." Pa scoffs, then sips his wine.

"Yeah, I heard it's quite grim at the Cape City Med hospital."

"Ja my child. The government stopped caring about their people a long time ago. They'd rather find ways to pocket the taxes than make it work for those who ignorantly voted for them." Pa scoffs.

I grab two plates from the cupboard and place them on the table, followed by two knives and forks, the pot of rice, sweet potatoes, green beans, and finally the *roemertopf*. Grace uses real apricots, grown here in the Ceres Valley, and a well-known South African brand of chutney for her chicken bake. It is heaven encrusted in a deep golden yumminess.

I look over all the food again. Grace was never one for waste, so why has she prepared for more than two?

"There's a lot of food here." I frown as I dish the food.

Pa doesn't look up from the table.

My stomach sinks into my feet. "Pa?"

"Hmpf." He sits back in his chair and folds his arms across his pudgy belly with an obscure gaze directed at me. "Raymond promised he might pop in."

Raymond, my delightful, A-class swindler of a brother was released from prison six months before I returned home. I haven't run in to him . . . yet. And I cross my fingers each time I make my way up the drive I never will.

"We'll leave his in the pot so it doesn't get cold, eh?" I ask.

Pa nods, and I silently beg that my sibling does not show his face.

I come around for dinner at least three times a week. Pa and I chat over a bottle of wine, take a walk through the vineyard, and then I go home.

"He's your brother, you know. You both share the same blood."

Why does Pa always have to push an agenda? "Not of my choosing." I regret the hateful words as they spill from my cheeky lips. "Sorry."

I haven't considered Raymond a part of my life for many years. My insides crawl at the thought that I share DNA with the guy.

"I love you, Pa. Let's not ruin a good evening, please?" I plead.

Pa's love for his *crim* son will always out shine the shadow of shame Raymond brought to my family. I'm no parent, so I couldn't understand, and all it does is stoke hot coals of disgust in my belly.

"Wait until you have children of your own one day." Pa aims a potato-laden fork at me.

"Not gonna happen." I try for humor by adding a smile.

Pa simply shakes his head and sighs.

We both dive into our food as though we've not eaten in days, and little more is said.

Pa pushes his empty plate away from him and leans back in his chair, one arm folded across his chest, the other holding his glass of wine. His bushy eyebrows bow, forming a crease between his eyes. "So, anyone important in your life?"

I choke on my last mouthful of chicken and beans as I shake my head. My eyes jump toward my glass of untouched wine. "Nothing better to discuss than why it's so important I have someone in my life?" The same cheekiness from earlier edges my tone.

A look of regret passes across his face. "Because love is important, Spooky." He shrugs. "Love brings meaning to our lives and fills those cold dark holes with light and warmth. Without it, the world would be far worse than it already is, and . . . it's been fourteen years."

I pick up my wine glass, sip, and consider the look of utter consternation on my father's face. My mind refuses to acknowledge the old memories aroused via my taste buds, but my body does not. I squirm uncomfortably in my chair. Dear God, I don't need this while sitting opposite my pa.

"I'm not going there. I will not waste my time on the past." I offer no further explanation and stand up from the table, collect and rinse the plates, then pack the washer.

"Not everything in life is black and white, Spook. It must be exhausting always running away."

I bite back my anger. Pa's last remark burns. "Not everything is as simple as turning grapes into wine either, Pa," I say over my shoulder and catch another, more worrying expression on the old man's face.

"Is there something you're not telling me? What's wrong?" I repeat the question he asked me on the day I arrived.

Pa frowns, shrugs, then refills our glasses.

Silently, we make our way down to the vines. It's a warm evening and I let go of the week's stress of working in the emergency department. I step off the lawn and into the field and relish the cool of the damp, fertile soil as it hugs my soles and toes. The air is a mixture of grape and roses. Its intoxicating aroma drifts up my nose and settles in my marrow as I turn my face toward the west.

"I missed this," I say, more to the sun than to Pa who stands beside me.

The humidity is high; it intensifies the reds and golds of the dozing sun. Motes bounce and dance from leaf to vine to leaf like little fairies hurrying home.

"It's not so simple to make a special wine either." Pa returns to the conversation I'd hoped he'd given up on.

I shake my head.

"He's stationed in Simon's Town." On his voice rides the faintest hope.

"Stationed?" I bite, not knowing what else to do with this man who refuses to see me grow old alone.

"Ja. He's a big do in the Navy. Some *groot kop* lieutenant who trains cadets and officers." Pa must have a lot of respect for the man if he calls him a head honcho. He's not one who easily doles out compliments.

"And you know this how?" I pin him down with the most potent doctor glare I can muster.

"I've always kept an eye on the poor boy. While I couldn't save him from Ibrahim, I managed to keep part of my promise to his father and mother . . ." His expression from earlier on returns, and is hard to ignore. But his words are simple, his tone flat, and their meaning carries the rampaging weight of a juggernaut.

"Keep what promise to his father and mother?"

"Ma and I knew his family. We had an obligation, one we both failed to fulfill."

3

It's a hot, windless, summer's day. My favorite.

I step out from the air-conditioned emergency department and into the inviting sun. Warmth and joy soak into my limbs. My exhaustion does not purely originate from being on my feet for the last six hours. Those stupid dreams. It's not easy to sleep peacefully when your body begs you to remember the touch of his skin or the warmth of his gaze . . .

A hooting, cursing taxi driver pulls me from my musings. I look left, then right, then left again, before crossing the road.

I've decided the few free minutes I'm afforded on a day shift are meant for ice crème. The emergency department can get hectic, depressing, and downright oppressive. Heaven knows it's been an emotional cesspool of late. With two groups of "allegedly" stolen children brought in by the police, it's hard not to want to know more. Where will they go once we've patched up the outside wounds? Have their parents been located? Will they find the healing help they need?

It hurts. But I can't allow myself to become attached or I will drown. Life is never easy or simple. I don't care what Pa says.

I make my way toward the vendor across the road from the hospital. He makes the best gelato from scratch. It's my pick-me-upper and in my opinion, is to ED, as chocolate is to the nasty shadows of soul-sucking despair.

"Know what you wanna order, *Sissi*?" The vendor leans forward on his counter.

"Honey crunch, please."

I smile as he places a large chunk of peanut brittle on the ice-cold metal plate and smothers it in honey before he begins to chop it up with his metal spatulas. He pauses to grab a small white jug and pours its contents of fresh crème over the delicious concoction and begins to mix. This is probably the best part of eating it—watching the dessert being made. The process fills me with a sense of happiness, not to mention how special and unique the taste is.

The concoction immediately freezes, and he spreads it out thinly across the plate. I look on like a child who's been promised a trip through a chocolate factory as this genius creates edible art right before my eyes.

With the skill of a master chef, the guy scoops up

the frozen delight with his spatula then places the four perfectly rolled portions in a cone and hands it to me.

A strange tingle slithers its way up my back as I reach for my dessert. I ignore it, pay for my portion of heaven, and turn to walk over to the large fig tree across the way. Its broad branches and cool shade beckon me.

But instead of a fig tree, I find myself staring into a pair of large brown eyes. Eyes I'd dreamt of for months after my disastrous sixteenth birthday.

My blood drains from my head and congeals in my toes. My lips turn to ice, and it's not from the dessert I've dropped on the damn ground. My heart somer- saults and ice-cold sweat stains my scrubs and trickles down my forehead.

Words I've desperately tried to ignore echo in my head.

There be a time for all tha things in dis world, and now be yours.

There, under the old fig, stands the boy who kissed me on my sweet sixteenth birthday, now a man. The one kiss it took years to forget. *Except I never did.*

. . . for there beneet tha twisted arms of weesdom waits peace, waits trust, waits harmony and your foreva lov . . .

The witch's voice drifts off with the ocean breeze, pulling me back into the heart and mind of my sixteen- year-old self.

Staring at me is the man who even now holds the key to my heart, and who has plagued my peaceful sleep of late. The same one who was dragged away by his angry family, ashamed and shunned. But also, the boy who shunned me in return.

There beneath the ancient welcoming arms of the old tree stands Thomas Campbell in his beautiful summer white Navy uniform. The starched material is so stark against his delicious olive skin, and the few rays of sunlight filtering through the leaves highlight the reddish hue to his crop-cut hair. His eyes draw me in, just as they did fourteen years ago. Deep pools of inviting chocolate, with hints of gold.

The Rochelle of fourteen years ago takes control of the me now standing in stained scrubs, ice crème melting on my shoes, simply staring like a lobotomized zombie. Not moving, just gawking as an emotional steam train knocks me out of my socks.

My mind's a jumble with questions. My emotions race uncontrollably through my veins. Surprise, fear, dread, and weirdly, happiness are all causing my head to spin like the swing ride at a carnival.

His mouth opens, and from it spills a single word. "Rochelle."

His voice has deepened, and its bass resonates against the ice façade it took me years to build around my disabled heart.

I want to cry. I want to scream. I want to say so many unsaid things, but my words sit like sticky toffee on the roof of my mouth, and my thoughts taper to a standstill as though caught in a tide of sludge.

He reaches out for me, his fingers long and elegant.

I can't breathe.

He takes a step closer.

There is enough distance between him and me that groups of people can walk between us, oblivious to the drama unfolding on this sad summer day.

He'd destroyed my innocent belief in love.

"Please," he pleads.

I take a step back.

I'd thought we'd shared something special, something like Ma and Pa. But it was soon clear, after countless returned letters, unanswered messages, him snubbing me when I'd caught a bus to his school—I was just an embarrassment. Everything he had done, or rather, hadn't done made me believe what happened was a mistake. That I was a desperate little white girl with nothing better to do.

And though we'd only shared one kiss, it was a kiss which had sealed my fate.

He takes another step toward me and I do the only thing my shattered sixteen-year-old heart is capable of.

I turn and run.

I return to work.

I work until my soul passes out. Until my synapses refuse to shoot impulses and my heart lays panting on the floor of my chest cavity. I break the rules and stay on for a second shift to ensure I'll never feel a thing again, ever, and to remind myself why I'm happy being single. Then I drag my aching body home and cry myself to sleep. Is it possible to hurt this much after all this time?

Yes! My sixteen-year-old heart screams as my thirty-year-old fractured soul consoles it.

Many people can have many loves, but for me, there was only ever one. After him, there was never room for another.

———

THOMAS'S HEART plummeted into his toes as Rochelle sprinted away from him and across the street, a minibus taxi only just missing her.

"*Voertsek umfazi!*" yelled the driver, cursing her as he hung from the window.

A small part of his heart sighed in relief that he hadn't walked up to her the other afternoon. But, for the most part, the tiny pieces of his heart he'd spent years gluing back together lay in a heap of burnt ash in the soles of his shoes.

He looked on as she disappeared around the next corner toward the hospital situated behind the rows of holiday apartments sprinkled along the esplanade.

He wanted to believe it was shock at seeing him again after all this time. But the blatant hurt painted across her face and the way her skin had turned grey told him it was a mixture of anger, fear, and rejection he'd awoken. After all these years, the connection and the hurt they'd both experienced that night had never faded, but merely hidden away.

Thomas heart hammered for him to run after her, but his mind told him to stay put, and yet another voice, one he believed he'd conquered the day he'd walked away from his abusive past, reminded him, *You, are a half-bred bastard. Who would ever love you?*

Thomas made his way along the quay.

The sun reflected off the turquoise waves, creating the illusion of water sprites dancing across its crystalline surface. Couples and families strolled up and down the boardwalk, others still picnicking on rugs spread out over the lush green lawn beneath trees and umbrellas. Thomas envied their happiness as he clung to his pain.

His phone vibrated, preventing Thomas from feeling sorrier for himself than he already did. It was an SMS from headquarters.

Another summons. He was an instructor and had not been active in duty for a while, but the rear admiral wanted his presence in the training exercise. One which dealt with a grave matter he'd thought resolved. Apparently not, and he couldn't have asked for it at a better time. There was nothing like hard work to distract from emotional turmoil.

4

I SWIM IN A LAKE OF MOLTEN GOLD AND DARK CHOCOLATE
as searing, hot lips trace a line across my jaw, down my
neck, and find my breasts. Strong, large hands glide
over my naked belly and slip between my thighs . . .

Thomas! an angry voice calls. Hard hands rip us
apart and I wake up, startled.

A roaring, enraged ocean drags me back to the
present as it crunches away at the sand on the beach,
spurred on by gale-force winds which bump and
thump against my doors and windows.

The doctor has arrived—the familiar southeasterly
winds which swoop down and rinse the pollution from
the Cape sky. Oh, how I wish it would blow away my
sodding broken heart too!

It's a miserable Friday and my first day off in a
week. Pa's left numerous messages on my phone. I've

sent him an SMS, telling him the emergency department is understaffed, which it is.

I've stitched up numerous gunshot wounds and drunken spouses and partners cut with the sharp end of broken bottles at local *shebeens*. And when the world couldn't get any darker, another lot of stolen children were rushed in. This time they were found in a dilapidated warehouse, a tip-off leading the police to their whereabouts before they were whisked off on a boat to face unimaginable horrors. One of the constables involved in the raid presented with a minor gunshot wound.

It's almost hilarious how the law forbids civilians to own handguns, yet it's as simple as driving to a street corner with fifty bucks and you can get yourself an automatic rifle.

It was gut-wrenching tending to the frail, tiny people with eyes who'd seen more darkness in their short lives than a battle-hardened soldier. Each child was accompanied by a police officer or social worker, and once their treatment was signed off by the unit manager, they were summarily escorted out to waiting vehicles and taken to goodness knows where.

"Do their parents know?" I'd asked one stern-looking officer, no longer able to play ignorant, and received a severe frown in reply.

I'd wanted to press for more answers, but I had to remind myself that I cannot get involved, even if the human part of me screamed to demand a reply.

I swing my legs off the bed and reach with my arms above my head as I stretch out the stiff weariness residing in my muscles.

Today, I have no more excuses. I'll have to drive up. Pa's waiting, and worried. As for me? I'm a frazzled human ball of messed emotions. So much for working myself to the bone.

I leave for *Nooitgedacht* just before lunch. I get into the double-cab *bakkie* I purchased at Pa's insistence. I'm grateful I listened to him as the wind tosses my four-by-four across the quiet highway like an autumn leaf. Anything smaller, and I'd be lying upside down on my roof on the side of the road.

I drive into the open garage. Pa pulls closed the door. He doesn't believe in electric-door motors, only good old-fashioned manpower and great big brass locks.

"You're sleeping here tonight. No arguments." He points a finger at me, then motions for us to go into the house through the connecting door.

"Grace has made the bed. She's found some toiletries. They're in your room and there are some old pajamas, jeans, and shirts from your cupboard."

I give him a "what the heck" look.

"I don't waste. Knew they'd come in handy some-day. See now." He points in the direction of my room.

"She still here? I want to thank her."

He shrugs and moves past me to the kitchen. "I sent her home early. God knows this wind is worse than usual. The vines are copping a pounding, and I only pray her tin shanty in that unscrupulous township remains standing after this one has passed. It gets worse every time."

"I thought she'd already be living in her government grant home?"

"Ha! Please. Our president is as bad as the ones up north, if not worse. Stolen billions for herself and her *tjommies*! Those friends of hers sit back and laugh like fat cats. The world smiles and waves, thinking our rainbow nation is one huge success story. Little do they know, not a single home has been built for our people in the last decade."

We make our way to the kitchen. The banshee wind screeches around the corners of the house, beating the vines, the windows, and the trees as though to confirm Pa's fear.

"Sit, Spooky. You have Casper rings under your eyes. You can't have them work you into the ground like this. It might be South Africa, but you still have rights. Or was it of your choosing?"

I turn my head away to avoid him seeing the truth on my face. I can't lie. Never could, and Pa has always read me like a book.

He dishes up the oxtail smothered in a red wine sauce. My stomach gurgles with joy and my mouth waters. No wonder he's become so portly. Grace has fed him only foods from heaven by the looks of it.

I cup the plate and take a deep whiff. "Ahh. Delish." It'll be my first decent meal in a week.

He pours our wine. It's as dark and rich as the sumptuous food.

"Let's pray." He takes my hand before I can pull it away.

"Geseende Vader. Ons dank u vir die voorreg wat hier voor ons op die tafel le . . ."

I refuse to close my eyes. I've been angry at Pa's god for a long time.

"Amen."

We eat in silence.

After a while, Pa surfaces from his second helping. "It's not God's fault, Spook."

I don't look up from my plate.

"I was angry too after he took your mother, and angrier still when they shunned your brother instead of helping me pray for his redemption. But then he showed me how he'd saved her from so much pain and suffering and that he had a plan for your brother. It's all about faith, Spooky."

"No amount of faith could save a person from cancer, Pa, and I won't begin to discuss the amount of pain she suffered." My words are sharp, and I instantly regret them. I decide not to mention my crim brother.

"Yes, my girl. I miss her every day and every night. Every time I look at you, and every morning I wake up alone in bed. But I know she is waiting for me. Love is about keeping the faith even when you want to believe there is no hope. It's the life jacket which keeps you from drowning while you're suffering through the storm. You don't have to believe in any god to know that."

"It's not only Mom who he deserted, Pa. I've seen too much, lost too many to ever feel differently." I can't look at him. If I do, I will cry. Instead I keep my eyes glued to my food. The thick, savory gravy, and sticky, juicy oxtail flesh, with its hints of thyme and aged red wine, soothe me. The sweet potato and red onion fill the hollow settling in my stomach.

"Food might not heal an aching heart, but it sure as hell sticks a fat Band-Aid on it. I don't care what any dietician or health guru thinks, but a large dish of love-filled, homemade food, and decent wine always hit the spot. Hey, Spooky?" Pa leans back and rubs his belly. He's so good at steering a dangerous conversation into calmer waters.

I smile, but still can't meet his gaze.

"Ice crème does the same," I mutter.

I haven't returned to the vendor in over a week.

Chicken.

Yes, I am.

————

"Lieutenant Campbell!" Thomas's admin officer calls.

Her coffee and crème complexion complement her tight black pencil skirt, matched with a shapely-cut white blouse. Janet Malherbe had most of the training base panting after her, though she only ever paid the female officers and cadets any notice. She was a woman with a steely determination and managed him and his office like a well-oiled ship. Outside of work she was a good friend and co-conspirator when it came to enjoying a fine whiskey.

"Sorry, Janet."

"*Sjoe*! But you were miles away, *ne*'? Come, it's time for your two o'clock planning exercise. Oh, and this came. Looks important." She handed him a registered letter pinched between two slim fingers which ended in sharp, blood-red nails. No other civilian employee dared to talk to him the way she did.

"Thanks. I'll get to it later." He dropped the letter on his desk and grabbed his hat and laptop.

When his frigate retired, Thomas had resisted a change to the maritime warfare school. But his role as a Navy specialist trainer in intelligence had been a welcome change—until now.

He'd heard whispers of pirates and illegal trafficking, but he'd never imagined it would be as bad as this. While all sources had pointed to it being a North African issue, not once had any of them ever realized it was occurring right off the shores of their own South Africa.

A car waited outside to drive him the short distance from the training facility to headquarters. The few silent moments in the back seat were enough time to envision a pair of sea-green eyes and strawberry-coated lips. They'd haunted his sleep every night this week.

Thomas walked into the conference room, saluted his superiors and fellow officers, then took his seat at the same time as he pushed his truest desire back into the darkest corner of himself.

A man Thomas knew to be in his early fifties, with hair as white as their formal uniforms, and eyes as dark as a stormy ocean, stood at the head of the table.

"Right, we have much to discuss." Rear Admiral Jonathan Penlevan leaned forward on the table with balled fists. "We've received more intel since our last exercise. Details are slim and grim, but it's time for the Navy to jump in. As you were informed at the previous meeting, a tip was given to the coast guard a month ago about some fishing boats carrying illegal cargo," the rear admiral explained as he turned toward his personal assistant. The young man dressed in a neat navy uniform stepped up to the table to manage the projector screen, and clicked the mouse beside the laptop. A map of the entire west coast of Africa popped up.

"At first it was thought to be drugs being carted to and from Nigeria. And the coast guard had assured us they had it under control. But they had seriously over-estimated their understaffed situation and had to call in the Navy when one of the boats had sent out an SOS *here*." He clicked his mouse, highlighting an area of ocean off the coast of Cape Town. "We've received orders from parliament house. As you all know, it was not drugs which were being transported, but humans and stolen antiquities. The children, as young as three and up to the ages of sixteen, were rescued off the sinking vessel. Many of them have been identified as the children who've been reported as kidnapped, or missing over the last months."

Another click, and a collage of horror spread across the screen. The images depicted dehydrated, emaciated children standing in their own filth.

"And if any of you believe *this* to be horrendous, I advise you to page two of the document."

Thomas scanned the page. Bile etched its way up his esophagus. The testimonies of the older children were enough to sicken the strongest of battle-worn soldiers.

"We have reason to believe that a gang of as yet unknowns, who are grooming and kidnapping the victims, are based right here in Simon's Town."

The information shook Thomas deeper than he'd care to admit.

"Questions," the rear admiral ordered.

"Yes, sir." Thomas stood, hands folded neatly behind his back. "May I ask why my presence has been requested? I've not sailed in months."

An all-knowing glance crossed the admiral's face. "It was with great sadness that we were notified of Lieutenant Mashabele's sudden passing a week ago. While we have other active first mates, there are none with your experience in intelligence. You'll not be returned to active duty on a ship, but you've been sent here to assist in the planning aspects of this operation."

He nodded curtly and Thomas relaxed a little.

The operation began in earnest with directives outlined and orders given. Thomas enjoyed the challenge it proffered but hated the fact they were striving to save young lives from the clutches of monsters. They were evildoers he'd gladly send to Davey Jones' locker.

Work began to draw to a close as the rear admiral stood.

"Thank you for your input today, Lieutenant." His commanding officer made a point of greeting Thomas as his assistant collected his laptop and paperwork.

Thomas rose, and saluted along with the other officers as the man exited and the strategy meeting ended.

Thomas began to collect his notes when his gaze caught on the photograph of a little boy, no older than he had been when he'd lost his parents. The child had bruises across one cheek and was dressed in filthy clothes a size too big. Something in the toddler's eyes drew him back to a night long ago—one he'd thought buried and forgotten.

Ibrahim had had him standing in the back garden, in only his underwear, reciting a phrase from a book he now detested.

The wind had howled and the cold had sliced through his skinny ten-year-old body, but he had not been allowed to return to the warmth of his bed or Ibrahim would've taken to him with the belt.

It was one of the many punishments that had been doled out. Punishment for not being pure. Punishment for being born . . .

To hell with those memories. They served only to cloud his mind in bitterness.

He shook his head, packed his device and notes into his satchel, and left.

———

THOMAS STEPPED out into the sharp summer sun and turned his face upward. The scorching rays washed away the demons which had arisen, and he smiled. Life was good now, and he would see to it that it would be good for the rescued children as well.

Thomas declined the car waiting to take him back to his office. He needed fresh air and time to think. He pulled his cap tighter over his head. The wind still howled across the Cape. Thankfully the buildings shielded him from some of its violent gusts. But every so often, he found himself trotting along the sidewalk like a crab as the gale bullied him and other pedestrians making their way to their various destinations.

He walked through the retractable glass doors of his office building and attempted to return to business.

His phone vibrated in his left pant pocket. He pulled it out.

Ibrahim, again? What did the man want? Why, after so many years, was he requesting for Thomas to come over for "conversation and some of Auntie's home-brewed tea?"

"Fukkit!" He dropped his phone on his desk.

"And now? Who's pissed on your battery?" Janet came to stand at the door of his office.

"It's bloody Ibrahim."

"Eish, what does he want?" She nodded toward the device.

"Dunno. But the man always had an agenda. I owe him nothing."

"*Ja.* But I don't think that's all that's on your mind, Lieutenant." Janet hit the nail on the head.

He was battling to cope with running into Rochelle after all these years. That was another part of his life he'd locked away with all the ugliness of his childhood.

"Ghost from the past." He waved off her comment and sat. Any hope he'd harbored of rekindling the spark lit long ago had been crushed that fateful lunchtime. Why had it all unfolded so badly?

"A girl?"

Thomas nodded.

"You know you can tell me anything, boss." Janet closed his door and came to sit in the chair opposite him. Her sharp demeanor had softened. She was a good friend and had often played the role of confidant over the years.

"I told you once about a girl I kissed as a young boy," he reminded her.

"*Ja*, I remember. The wine farmer's daughter."

"Well, she's back and we ran into each other a week ago. She'd not been happy to see me—not as happy as I was to see her, that's for sure." The memory of her bright eyes staring at him in shock still stung like the business end of an angry hornet.

His mind was a jumble of questions, and his heart throbbed like a drunken sailor's head. "The last time I saw such pain on her face was the day she'd stood waiting outside my school—the day I had to turn my back on her to protect us both from my uncle."

"*Bliksem!* The universe has really handed you a bitch-slap," Janet responded in her usual straightforward manner.

Thomas sighed as the weight of the world pushed down on his shoulders. "If only I'd been stronger, stood up to Ibrahim and Trish, perhaps . . ."

"*Ai,* Lieutenant. We both know why that didn't happen and it wasn't 'cause you were weak, *ne*'." Janet shook her head.

"But they had, in their own twisted way, been right, Janet. I'm a half-breed with one foot rooted in Cape Malay heritage and the other in second-generation Scottish DNA."

"And what do you think I am? We all have a mixture of everyone who's ever come to this country running through our veins. People like Ibrahim and

Trish are too full of themselves and their hypocritical bullshit to understand that." Janet's gaze turned to fire. "That's why he hid the truth of your parents from you. He is terrified of the strength inside of your heart. He will never be the man you are."

Ibrahim Abad had refused to divulge any information about Thomas's parents, only ever telling him he was a colonial, *kaffir*, half-breed. A sin in the eyes of his uncle's god.

"Look. The way I see it, we all cross each other's paths for a reason. It's up to us what we do with it, *ne'*." Janet stood, hands on her hips. "I'll go make us a cup of coffee. You have a full inbox; best get to it. Maybe we can chat some more over a drink tonight?"

"Ja." Thomas nodded as she left him to his own thoughts, and his work.

He unpacked his laptop, he pondered his childhood.

He'd been so small, so afraid. The night of his parents' deaths was showered in the fog and confusion of the traumatized mind of a small child.

Thomas had searched for evidence of them when he'd turned eighteen, but all documentation pertaining to his birth and his mother had mysteriously vanished. His uncle's reach was deep. The only papers he could find were a registration of a guardian to a child by the name of Thomas Andrew Campbell.

What did it matter? His parents had long since turned to dust and distant memories. And while he knew his uncle hid many truths from him, Thomas had eventually decided to leave the unknown behind him and look to the future—his only escape from years of abuse.

The first time his life had touched hope was that night fourteen years ago. His fingers stroked his lips as his mind returned to Rochelle.

Should he seek her out? Explain why he'd shunned her that day? If only to tell her he was deeply sorry? He wouldn't bother mentioning he'd hurt as much as she had, or that he'd dreamed of her for months, even years, after. In those night time wonderings, he'd imagined glimpses of her. Images his subconscious had conjured, images which had kept him going through the worst of times. There were days when it felt hard to breathe at the thought of never seeing her again or touching her. Often the dreams had felt so surreal he'd thought that . . . if he could reach out to her, speak to her, hold her . . . he'd do just that.

They'd eventually stopped—until a month ago.

She obviously worked at the hospital, but it would not be a good idea to approach her there. He'd wait for her beneath the fig tree.

He hadn't gone back to his tree since that afternoon. Would she return? He'd seen her there more than once before she'd noticed him.

No use regretting it now. He had to make things right—to take away her hurt so they both could carry on with their lives in their own way.

A notification popped up on his computer screen as Janet returned with a steaming mug of coffee. Thomas pushed Rochelle and his scattered emotions to the back of his mind.

———

WELL FOR ONCE, something other than my heart aches. Lunch ran into dinner and another bottle of wine. Grace had cooked enough for an army, obviously expecting my wayward sibling to join. Pa and I sat reminiscing about days when Ma was around, and Raymond wasn't a rotten apple. I still can't grasp how two children birthed from the same loins, with the same genes, could turn out so differently. One successful, the other a criminal.

We laughed about *Ouma* and the hornets' nest. We cried when we remembered sprinkling Ma's ashes over the vineyard.

Eventually, as the old cuckoo clock chimed some ungodly hour, Pa rubbed his eyes and declared, "Right. It's this old man's bedtime."

I packed the last of the dishes into the washer as he stood to leave.

But he stopped and turned back. "Spook?"

"Yes, Pa?" The seriousness of his voice had struck a chord.

"Would you forgive your old man a secret or two when the time comes?"

The question had failed to slice through my wine-induced fog at the time and I'd simply nodded. But it comes thundering back like a herd of angry bull elephants now.

What did he mean? Or was it simply nostalgia and too much wine on his part?

Agh, honestly, I am overthinking it all.

Water. I need to hydrate.

I sit up, slowly. Ugh, that's not good. I rub the sides of my throbbing skull with the palms of my hands. Then, like an arthritic sloth, I stand. My legs wobble. I catch my reflection in the dressing table mirror. Dear Lord, I'm a mess. My hair looks like Nina from Daleen Mathee's *Fiela se kind*. My stomach twists, and bile sours the back of my throat. I just had to have that second bottle, didn't I?

"Morning, Spooky!" Pa bursts into my room, and my head explodes. He hands me the glass of his famous *babalas* fixer as he pulls open my curtains.

"Ouch." I rub the back of my neck and head.

I grip the concoction of black grapes, a paracetamol powder, and some other stuff I forget, in my hand. It works as fast and efficiently as a 0.9 percent lactated ringer's solution IV after a heavy night of drinking the fermented fruits of Bacchus. It's the best hangover drink that exists.

"*Ja*, well, any fool could have told you a second bottle was bound to kick you in the arse. Come. I have a *lekka* breakfast on the stove. You need some oily protein to line that soured stomach of yours."

My innards churn at the mention of food.

He leaves me to it. I down the thick, purple sludge, gag, and swallow. I need some fresh air, and walk over to the window. The wind is still blowing like there's no tomorrow. I open it a smidge and allow the cool mountain gale to wash over me.

Head clearer, I stumble down the passage to the kitchen. The sweet savory smell of bacon drizzled in golden syrup with poached eggs meets me halfway. My stomach flips, and I run for the loo.

5

I smile as Pa wipes the yolk and grease off his plate with a slice of sourdough bread. He shoves it in his mouth, swallows, then licks his fingers off like a cat lapping up every last drop of crème in its bowl.

"Now that was a good feed." He never wastes a thing.

I manage an egg. That's as far as I am willing to push my luck. The second glass of *babalas* fixer, followed by a mug of steaming peppermint tea, works wonders, and my head feels clearer than it did when I woke up.

"They weren't short-staffed were they, Spook?"

"No." I sip my tea.

"Did you go look for him?"

"No." I down my tea and give my father a once-over. "How do you know it's Thomas?"

Pa smiles. "It's painted across your face. You're like an open book, my child."

"Why Thomas, Pa? I was sixteen. Surely no one falls in love after a single kiss. And didn't you and Ma cop loads of *kak* because he was . . . was . . ." I can't say it.

"Because he's seen as a colored? Ai, Spook, you should know better!" He leans forward and places his aged, calloused hands on my shoulders.

"I should have told you that night, but Ibrahim Abad stirred up such a ruckus, and what with the promise I'd made and . . . I thought it best left alone, and then Ma . . . Agh, today is as good a day as any I suppose."

"Told me what? And what promise?"

"That Ma and I were never against the idea of the two of you. We knew how poorly Abad treated that young boy." A look of regret and shame passes across his face. "We knew his parents before . . ." Pa's voice drifts off as it often does when he loses himself in thoughts of the past.

"Before what?"

"His parents were killed. It was a terrible thing." Pa shakes his head, then stands and collects the dishes. "We always wondered if he wasn't behind it," Pa says over his shoulder.

"Ibrahim Abad?" I say, more in a whisper, not sure who it is I'm afraid of overhearing our conversation.

"Yes. It was a hijacking. But in hindsight . . ."

"Why would he? What was his motive? And what promise?" I push before Pa loses himself to his thoughts once more.

He doesn't answer immediately, but instead, opens the tap and rinses the plates before stacking them in the washer.

"Pa?"

He turns around, his blue eyes shrouded in secrets. "It's a well-known and unproven fact that Abad and his boys are involved in crime."

"But he sits on the South Oversight Based Area of the Cape Town municipality portfolio. How is it possible that—"

"He is involved in crime?" The irony in Pa's voice is unmissable. "The same way our president lays down with the corrupt Tipta family and calls it international relations."

There are few municipalities which aren't rife with corruption these days, although most believe Cape Town to be one of the better ones.

"What sort of crime, Pa? And. What. Promise?"

"A promise I can't share with you yet. And the sort of crime which one prefers to ignore. The sort it took a specialized policeman such as Thomas's father to track down, but—"

"They got to him first." My voice quakes. "Does he know? Surely, he would?"

"I doubt it. No one dares say a word for fear of . . . He is free of Ibrahim now. That is all that matters."

"But surely Thomas has a right to know about his parents?" The agitation in my tone causes my voice to rise an octave.

I can see it in the old man's eyes. There is more to this tale than he is telling me. But I am battling with what he has already shared.

"Yes, he'll know soon enough. A promise is a promise."

I watch, gobsmacked, not sure what to make of this new information, as Pa finishes the dishes.

"Come, I have something for you."

I have no idea what Pa is on about, but I follow him to the formal lounge. It was Ma's pride and joy, filled with all the furniture passed down through the generations. Hand-carved tables and chairs, not the most comfortable to sit on but beautiful to look at. There's a double-seated *riempies* chair, the frame made of carved and polished iron wood. It is threaded with cured kudu leather thongs woven for the seat. My great-great-grandpa made it with his own hands. Beside it sits an elaborately carved coffee table brought all the way from France when the Huguenots arrived. On the far side, over by the fireplace, stands her special - special. A show cabinet from England. Ma was as proudly English as Pa was proudly French-Dutch.

Inside, tucked neatly out of the reach of sticky fingers and dust motes, are fading black-and-white photos of great-great-grandparents, aunts, and uncles, along with crystal glasses and other trinkets, such as small teaspoons, and mine and Raymond's bronzed baby shoes. All of the items wait patiently to show off the memories they conjure.

Something inside of me shifts. My eyes find the cup. I've not so much as glanced at it since that awful night fourteen years ago—not since it glanced back at me on the afternoon I returned home. It is Pa's most precious possession, passed on to him by a great-aunt who'd not had any children of her own, leaving Pa as the eldest firstborn grandchild in the family.

Pa turns the small silver key, which always sits in the lock, and opens the glass cabinet door. He reaches inside and takes it out. "Remember this?"

He holds it out for me to take. I can't move. "What has this old thing got to do with . . . him?"

Pa considers the cup for a moment. "It's not an old thing, Spook. It's a keepsake and it's special."

Its polished pewter complexion glints as a ray of sunshine peers through the window behind him and bounces off its buffed surface.

"I know it reminds you of that night. It's an heirloom which has been in the Le Roux family since the days the Huguenots left France for the shores of Cape Town. And it's been passed down from family member to family member over the decades."

"I'm not the eldest, Pa."

He ignores me and instead, turns it and reads the inscription. "*Le vin est la preuve que dieu nous aime et aime nous voir heureux."* His French is somewhat tainted by his accent.

"What does it mean?" I reluctantly take the cup from him.

"Wine is proof that God loves us and loves to see us happy." He smiles.

I try not to blink, but the tears run anyway.

"Agh, I'm not doing this to hurt or upset you. You know Ma and I never blamed you, nor did we have any problems with you enjoying your first kiss."

My cheeks heat. Pa has always been a man who calls it as he sees it.

"The thing is, there is a story that goes with this cup. A story older than the vines in those fields. A bit of a superstition, if you will. Come, let's go sit down." He closes and locks the cabinet door, then puts his arm around me, and we walk to the kitchen.

I eye the cup standing in the middle of the kitchen table.

"It wasn't your Great Grand *Ouma* who passed this down to her firstborn."

I look up surprised. "I assumed . . ."

"Ah, assumption. Such a needless thought. No, Spooky. The cup chooses its home. It chose you that night, just as it chose me so many years ago."

Skepticism surfs my thoughts as I glance from the cup to my pa.

"It was your Great Aunt Sophie who handed it

down to me one Sunday after church. She believed it had brought every Le Roux their one true love."

"Like you and Ma?" I scoff, and Pa frowns.

"Yes, like me and your Ma. Don't you look at me like that, my girl! I have all my screws bolted tight inside my head." Pa points his finger at his temple, purses his lips, and looks at me.

"You are such a romantic." I reach for the cup, clasp its stem between my thumb and forefinger, and twirl it. "So, what you're telling me is that you only love Ma because of this cup?" My tone drips with sarcasm.

"Now listen to me, young lady. Do I strike you as a fool? I loved your mother from the moment I first saw her."

"And when was the first time you saw Ma?"

"The day Aunt Sophie asked me to please take the cup in for its monthly polish at the old antique store, which your *Oupa* owned, and where your Ma used to work."

I think back on the night I met Thomas. I could have easily grabbed a glass from the kitchen table. But instead, I'd wanted to be fancy and grabbed the cup from my mother's cabinet. Something about its shiny surface and twisted stem had called to me.

"You see, it was meant to be." His eyes sparkle with the wonderment of a small child. "Tell me, Spook, that night when he kissed you—did you feel it?"

I fold my arms across my chest. Does my father honestly expect me to believe the silly superstition?

But I know exactly what he is asking about. I remember it as though it happened yesterday. The tingle, the burn, the searing, hot knife tip which poked at my soul. The moment a piece of both our hearts fused together, like a gem set in gold for all eternity.

Pa smiles knowingly. "There's something to be said about fate holding true love's hand."

"Pa, now you're reaching."

"*Ai*, Spook. For some there are many loves. But, for a select few, there is the blessing and the burden of loving only one, eternally. Why've you never held onto a boy since? None of them measured up, did they? Even the handsome, clever *poophols* you worked with."

"That's low, Pa, even for you. They weren't all assholes. They were simply lacking in character."

We both burst out laughing.

Pa calms after a while, takes a deep breath, and places a warm hand on my shoulder. "But it happened. I know it did. Ma and I saw it in your eyes. Just as it shone brightly in our own. It's not magic, Spook. It's meant to be."

He smiles, his eyes dreamy and far away. Memories of Ma?

He pushes the cup toward me. "It's yours. Has been for a long time."

I don't know what to do, so I say the only thing that might get me out of this awkward moment. "I need caffeine."

I put the cup upstairs in my room, then return to the kitchen to make coffee.

"Even if what you're saying is true, it was over before it started. He and his uncle made sure of that." I fill the kettle and place it back on its element, flicking the switch. "Coffee?"

"*Ja,* but not that dust that Grace loves to drink. Here, let me make us a proper brew." Pa pushes me toward a chair. "Look, I didn't agree with how that *blerrie* Ibrahim reacted back then, but there was little I could do. He is a powerful man. But I knew one day, you and Thomas would find one another when the time was right, and that old coot could do nothing about it."

I watch as he reaches into the cupboard above and pulls out a hessian bag with coffee beans in it. He lifts it to his face. "Mmmm *lekka.*" He turns. "And here you are. You haven't been back a month and the two of you have found each other. So perhaps, my dear, it's time you stop your nonsense? Think how that poor boy must have felt. Did you know how badly his uncle and aunt treated him?"

I shake my head.

"No, of course you didn't, and I'm sure he would have hated it if you did. They treated him worse than the filth beneath their feet. It was a well-known fact Ibrahim saw him as abhorrent because of his mixed race. But that's past. The point is, he had as little control over the situation as you did, my dear."

Pa's words call back my headache. I was so young and innocent in the ways of the world. I had no idea how to deal with my broken heart back then and so I simply decided to ignore it. To hide it beneath hours of studying and work, only for it to resurface now and remind me that I still have no idea how to deal with it. "Is he in danger from his uncle?" I'm not sure why I ask, but something in me has to know.

Pa stops grinding the beans and sighs deeply. "Perhaps, Spook. Though now, at least, he is able to protect and defend himself. But the time will come when all will be revealed, and until that day, I have no right to share his story with you."

His cryptic reply causes the hair on my arms and neck to rise up like the dead in a bad horror flick. "What do you mean?"

"That it's not my story to tell. Not to you, anyhow." He smiles in an attempt to soften his words.

And while I know he means no malice, I hate the feeling that there is something very important my pa is keeping from me.

6

THOMAS WAS DEEP IN PLANNING FOR HIS NEXT CLASS when the office phone beckoned with a sharp shrill. Janet was out, so Thomas clicked *save,* then reached for the receiver, pressing down on the button for his line.

"Good day. I'm looking for Lieutenant Campbell."

The deep voice struck a distant, hidden chord of familiarity inside the darkest recesses of Thomas's mind. "Good day, you're speaking to him. Who is this?"

"Ah, I'm not sure you remember me? It's Derrek Le Roux from Nooitgedacht Wineries."

The words knocked Thomas back into his chair. "Mr. Le Roux! Ah . . . err . . . is Rochelle okay?"

"She is fine. Although I do believe she pines for you in the same pitiful way you do for her. But, for now, I'd like to know if you've received the letter?"

Thomas heard the hint of excitement in the old man's voice. It seemed to catch, travelling down his back, all the way to his toes.

"Letter?"

"Yes, my boy. The registered letter from Bezuidenhout and Partners Law Firm."

Thomas reached forward and grabbed the unopened envelope he'd dropped on his desk and forgotten about. Normally, he'd waste no time in opening registered post. But what with the training exercise and Rochelle, his mind had not been focused.

"Erm, sorry, sir. No, I haven't."

Thomas pinched the receiver between his left shoulder and ear as he grabbed his letter opener and tore through the white paper of the envelope.

"Read it, and call me when you're ready," Derrek said, and ended the call.

———

THOMAS GRITTED his teeth and knocked on the front door of Ibrahim Abad's house. This was not the way he'd intended to spend his Saturday.

He'd pondered the relevance, no, the sheer impact the contents of the letter delivered to his life, over half a bottle of Johnny Blue the previous night. He'd thought of calling Janet to share his discovery, but she had other plans and he wasn't quite ready to reveal the news to anyone yet.

The letter was in fact a will, leaving him all his parents' worldly possessions. The sort of thing a lawyer reads out to those remaining behind after the funeral, except theirs was not. He couldn't even remember attending a funeral, or was that because Ibrahim hadn't taken him? Now he thought about it, he had no idea where his parents were buried. All he could remember was the rain, and the fear.

Thomas escaped the foggy memories of so long ago and focused on the papers in his possession. A second envelope inside the registered one had contained a letter with instructions and two sets of keys, from Derrek Le Roux.

That morning, he'd gone to inspect the house and some of the treasures in a hired storage garage. All bits and pieces of a life and family he'd once been a part of.

It had almost been too much to take in. His head had agreed with a slight throb.

It was time he put this greedy, conniving, corrupt man in his place. Then and only then could he move forward and allow himself to honor the things that mattered: his parents, his heritage, his reason for being here, and most importantly, who'd killed them.

Unlike the other houses, his aunt and uncle's front door was not barricaded by a six-foot wall or electric fence. Nor was their place of residence situated amidst the brightly colored houses of the Cape Malay community in the Bo-Kaap near the Mother city's center. Their front garden was well maintained, with two large oak trees spreading their branches across the neatly trimmed lawn.

Thomas had always suspected there was good reason why their house, unlike everyone else's, was safe from the unwanted visitations of thugs and thieves. While his uncle had always kept him hidden and locked away, he'd not missed the late-night drop by from hooded strangers, or the odd word dropped here or there.

Thomas's knuckles rapped on the door. He struggled to rein in his anger, but his grip was tenuous at best. Today, he would have it out with Ibrahim. Was the fact he'd just turned thirty and been made aware of his parents' small fortune the reason Ibrahim had left countless messages?

The door opened, and his Auntie Trish stood in the entrance. Her mouth puckered as though she'd bitten into a lemon and her gaze hardened as she nodded .

"Morning, Thomas. So nice of you to grace us with your presence. What brings you to our doorstep?" Her tone was cool, and dismissed any pretense of genuine concern.

"Morning, Trish. Ibrahim called me."

She would get no more than she offered.

Her blatant dislike of him had stopped cutting years ago, but he'd never forgotten the hurtful words and tongue-lashings she'd dealt out with glee while he'd lived under their roof. She'd never liked his mother and when Thomas came to live with them, she made sure he knew it.

Like most women in the tight-knit Cape Malay community, his aunt wore a long dress shirt over full-length pants with a scarf covering her head, all made from bright bold colors and trimmed in gold lace. She was short and plump, and reminded him of a penguin when she walked—so unlike her tall, skinny husband.

"Your uncle is in his study, awaiting you." She motioned with her hand toward the door down the far end of the passage.

Thomas nodded politely and walked into the house. Its old wooden floors creaked beneath his feet.

The hair on Thomas's neck stood at attention and his instinct was to turn and run. Dark, painful memories fought for place in his mind. Thomas shook his head and pushed them away, and instead clung to the memory of a pair of bright cyan-colored eyes. The same eyes which had kept him sane all those years ago in this very house.

Thomas tugged on the edge of his jacket. He'd worn his semi-formal whites. It was a Saturday, but he had a point to make, and in some strange, childish way, he felt safe clothed in his Navy bests.

"Ah, Thomas." Ibrahim looked up from reading as Thomas entered. He was the same reed-thin man he'd always been. Only now, Thomas was taller than he. Taller, broader, and wiser.

His uncle's hair had greyed, and the years sat etched in the corners of his eyes and mouth. But the devil still danced in his dark, demented eyes.

"Good of you to come." His voice had that lyrical tone to it—the one he'd always used on people of importance.

Thomas's instincts rebelled. Ibrahim stood and Thomas walked up to the desk and shook his uncle's hand. While he didn't deserve it, there was no need to disrespect him in his own home. Thomas would always take the high road.

"Trish, some tea please," Ibrahim said, then to Thomas, "Off to the base afterwards?"

"I won't be here long enough for tea." Thomas stiffly stepped back and eyed his uncle.

"I am pleased that you finally found the time to answer my messages, Thomas." Ibrahim's smirk stung like acid.

"What is it you want, Ibrahim?" Thomas knew exactly what his uncle wanted—had guessed it once he'd opened the letter from the attorney's office.

"To see how you were doing, my dear boy." The slithering tone Ibrahim used to try to show he cared pinched every nerve Thomas owned.

"What you actually mean to ask is if I have received any mail of interest lately?" Thomas pushed away the urge to allow his anger to get the better of him. Instead, he kept his face blank and forced his voice into a monotone.

Ibrahim's head whipped back as though Thomas had struck him. "Whatever would that be?" Ibrahim recovered and aimed two dark eyes right at Thomas.

"I'm sure you're itching to tell me, Uncle."

Two could play this game, and he'd learnt from the best.

With a dramatic sigh and waving of hands in the air, Ibrahim let go of some of his pretense. "Very well. You've recently turned thirty. Did you honestly believe I had no idea of your inheritance, Thomas?"

Ah, and there it was.

"I knew there would be a reason behind you trying so hard to reconnect after all these years." Thomas made sure to keep his face and voice void of emotion as he paced around his uncle's study.

It was one of the largest rooms in the house, with a dozen bookshelves lining the walls and priceless Persian carpets laid out across the wooden floor. Dozens of small and medium sculptures and expensive items decorated the room, ones Thomas had often thought belonged in a museum rather than here.

Thomas stopped in front of the bookcase. A gold-engraved spine stood out from all the others on the shelf. Thomas cautiously ran a finger over the cool leather. It had filled him with fear and bitterness as a child, but no longer. It was only a leather-bound cover hugging paper. Though its pages were considered by many of his uncle's faith to be holy, Thomas knew better. It was a belief Ibrahim had often used to browbeat him with. A book he'd been forced to study, and one he'd not read since leaving the Abads' house.

He turned to face his uncle.

The older man's eyebrow arched as he nodded toward the book. "It's yours. You conveniently left it here the day you ran away from us."

Thomas ignored the comment aimed to upset him. Ibrahim sat back down and balanced a sharp chin on steepled fingers. "What have you decided to do, Thomas?"

"With the book?" Thomas couldn't help himself as he watched frustration pace the width of his uncle's gaze.

"With that which is supposedly yours?"

Thomas paused, stretching out his reply as Ibrahim pursed his lips and shifted in his seat the way he did when he was getting impatient.

"Are you wanting to advise me as to what would be best?" Thomas etched his tone with a subtle sarcasm as he came to stand opposite Ibrahim, running an index finger along the carved edge of his uncle's large oak desk.

"I am your legal guardian, after all." Ibrahim's voice cut a long-ago wound Thomas thought no longer existed. His words were fuel to the smoldering coals of Thomas's anger. But instead of reacting, Thomas drew himself up to his full six foot and squared his shoulders.

"I've long since been of an age where you are no longer anything of mine. There's no lost love between us, Ibrahim. You're after my parents' money, aren't you?"

A flash of, was that dismay sprinting across Ibrahim's face as his cheeks blanched and his irises narrowed to the size of pinheads?

"Your father often worked from his home office . . ." Ibrahim swayed slightly from the topic, catching Thomas off guard.

"And you know this how?" As far as Thomas could remember, Ibrahim and Trish had only ever graced his parents with a single visit. A visit Trish had often mentioned. The day they had decided to remind Kasih, his mother, of her blatant blasphemy.

"Has it stood empty all these years?" Ibrahim leaned forward, his pupils enlarging as his fingers pinched the edge of the desk.

"The house?" Thomas feigned ignorance.

"Yes." Ibrahim's voice slid across the room like a python who'd spotted its prey.

"Why?"

"So, Derrek Le Roux sold all their belongings?"

Thomas considered the poorly hidden assumption within his uncle's words.

What was Ibrahim after? Thomas's instinct warned there was more to this than the small fortune he'd recently inherited.

He decided not to answer, and simply shrugged.

"Are you sure it's me who is after the money, and not him?" Danger flashed across the older man's gaze as he changed tactics.

Thomas tempered his rising anger. Derrek had sold nothing. In fact, at a cost to himself, he'd had Thomas's parents' possessions stored safely away. Ah, but Ibrahim was setting the trap. Thomas would not share the truth with the man as he consciously maneuvered around the snare.

"What is your interest in where my father worked from? And why do you want the pittance left to me when you have so much? Derrek warned me you might try to get your grubby paws on it. Aside from the house and the money, I have nothing of my parents."

"That damn *Boer*! He managed to keep his claws on what was rightfully mine! The house, all its belongings, were meant to be handed over to me. But no, some minor legal clause kept it from me, and all I got was a sniveling bastard brat!"

And there was the Ibrahim Thomas knew. And why the property? What was it about his father's study and its contents? Thomas struggled with emotions which threatened to flare up and cause him to lose his cool. He was obviously not meant to be part of the package; no wonder Ibrahim had treated him like a pavement special. Years of fear, hurt, and anger the likes of which Thomas had not yet known roiled in his stomach and pushed up his gullet. The bile burnt the back of his throat. But he refused to allow even a drop of it to show on his face or in his actions.

Instead, Thomas calmed the hurricane within as a vague memory slipped into the forefront of Thomas's mind.

A night, so very long ago, when he'd heard his mother scream, glass breaking, and after, the pretty lights of a police car. He remembered the broken window and the upturned state of the room his father had called his study. But the memory was vague, and Thomas wasn't sure if it was real or something his mind had conjured.

His uncle paused, took a deep breath, and when a knock sounded at the door, ground out, "Enter!"

Trish placed a gold-plated tray with slim-cut glass teacups on it and a tall matching teapot on the table between them. Ibrahim nodded, and she poured them each a cup before leaving, closing the door behind her.

"If you would care to sit, Thomas, I will explain." Ibrahim waved a hand toward a chair.

"There is no need for an explanation, Ibrahim."

"You will sit and you will obey me. I am your elder." His Uncles anger was getting the better of him once more, and a small part of Thomas enjoyed that, for once, his uncle was powerless and had no control over him.

Then it struck him. Ibrahim was desperate. "I have nothing more to say to you, Ibrahim."

"Then why come here?"

"To look you in the eye. To show you that you can never harm me again. To tell you that you will never see a cent of my parents' money, that you have no more say over me, or anything which is mine, or was theirs. That even if I saw you begging for scraps alongside the road, I'd first feed the dogs before thinking on you. Never call me again. Stay out of my way and my life." He made sure to keep his voice low but edged his tone with the punch of an iron fist.

Thomas swallowed back a smile when his uncle's hands trembled as his cheeks turned sallow and the old man plonked down into his chair.

"Thomas, please, surely we can find a way to . . ." Ibrahim tried for calm. "Fine! How much do you want for that rundown hovel?" The old man's determination returned with gusto as he stood back up.

Ibrahim's offer was as much a revelation as it was a surprise. There was definitely something about the house and the contents of his father's study that this man was after, but why?

"I'd sell it for one *Rand* to a hobo before I gave any of my family's possessions to you! I am Thomas Andrew Campbell, and you are nothing of mine. You never loved me as one of my blood should have. You abused the power you believed you had over me. You tried to sully anything that was pure and good and right about my parents. But you failed! I owe you nothing, old man. Nothing!"

Thomas exhaled deeply as he spun on his heel and

left, reminding himself that this would not be the last time Ibrahim Abad would approach him. For whatever reason, Thomas could not shake the uneasy suspicion that the old man would vehemently pursue what he was after until he got what he wanted.

7

I love Sunday mornings.

There's always been something special to me about waking up on a Sunday, realizing it's the beginning of a new week and getting to sleep in. Thankfully, I have no shifts until Tuesday.

What I don't like about *this* Sunday though, is the voice calling from the front hall. Raymond has come home. I drag myself from my bed, shower, and dress, then make my way toward the chattering voices in the kitchen.

"Yes, yes, Sis!"

I dodge his attempt at a hug, but not Pa's scowl.

"You stink, Raymond. When did you last take a bath?" I scrunch my nose at the acrid odor of cigarette smoke, and a smell I can only equate to the sour stench of week-old sweat or pee; it calls back a memory. Earlier in the week, a druggie had run in to the emergency department and bumped into me, he'd smelled the same. I hadn't seen his face thanks to a hoodie, but he'd quickly taken off when security appeared. I shake my head. Was Raymond back on drugs? Wouldn't surprise me in the least. But now was not the time to confront him on the rules concerning his parole.

"You tired of tents, dust, and play-play work? And what's this candy floss *kak* you've got in your hair?"

I swat away his hand as he criticizes the blue and pink hues I colored into my blond hair the same week I returned home.

"Leave her be, Raymond," Pa warns.

Raymond is six feet two and full of arrogant stupidness. He is also three years older than me.

"Yes, Bro. You tired of jail grub and inmates pinching your bum in the shower?" I can't help myself.

Pa smiles.

I make coffee, and Raymond's mouth spews less palaver.

It's easy to use his time in prison against him. A part of me cares about the narcissistic ass. But in all truth, I like Raymond Le Roux as much as I like dog poo stuck to the bottom of my shoe.

"So, what brings you this way?" I need to know, Raymond only shows his face when he is in trouble or wants money.

Pa gives me a look. I shrug, hand Pa his cup, and lean against the kitchen counter, sipping my coffee.

"Heard you were back. Thought I'd pop in and say *howzit*."

Yeah, right! "Where you staying?" Please not here. Pa is such a sucker for his crim son.

"In the city with a friend." He doesn't look up as he makes his own cuppa.

But I see it. The hooded *something* he is trying hard not to show. Pa may be blind to it, but I never was.

Pa's mouth opens and I know it's to invite him to stay here, but I stop him with a look and say, "Good."

Raymond glares at me. We've never gotten along. Even before he'd turned to a life of convenient crime and *dagga*, he was arrogant and selfish. He hurt my parents and used anyone he could. Still, Pa might see his faults, but at the end of the day, Raymond is his only son.

"What ever happened to that boy you kissed on your birthday?" Raymond asks out of the blue.

I almost choke on a mouthful of coffee.

"Why?" I snap as I shoot Pa a querying look.

"Agh, just asking hey. And you, Pa? You know everything about everyone and seriously now, you never used to hide the safe keys. What you got locked away in there?"

Pa sips his coffee, sighs, and look his son dead in the eye. "I never used to have a son with a criminal record."

I swallow hard. Never did I ever think Pa would say

something like that. I look back at Raymond. Something's going on.

"What are you up to, *boet*? I haven't seen Thomas in fourteen years and you've never been interested in the safe unless you wanted to shoot some fowl. I doubt Pa has either. What's he got that you want?" I accuse him.

"Geez, Shelly. Just asking, okay?"

"Don't call me that," I mumble.

Thankfully my brother takes his leave, realizing we won't be of any help.

To crown it all, he drops one last comment as he saunters to the front door. "I'm the oldest, *ne'*, Pa?"

"Last time I checked." Pa tries for humor.

"Then where's the cup?"

Pa laughs. "I love you, my son, but after that nonsense you pulled with the pyramid scheme, don't go telling yourself you're still in line to inherit a thing after your share was used to pay back your victims!"

Ten out of ten, Pa!

I don't like the look Raymond gives us as he storms out. Pa's shoulders slump and his skin turns a soft grey as he wipes the back of his hand across his eyes. I move toward the old man and wrap my arms around him. I can't imagine how much that must have hurt.

We finish our coffee in silence, after which I go to my room and pack my day bag, leaving a note of thanks and some money on my laundry basket for Grace.

The wind has died down, and dark clouds are

building on the horizon. Their bulging, mulberry-colored fists run a chill through my center. They warn of more than a summer storm.

I pick up the silly silver cup from my bedside table. For a split second, I am tempted to throw it in the trash, but a voice as soft as an angel's whispers, *No!*

It's the one link which remains, not only to my heritage, rich in history and tales, but also to him. My fingers trace my lips, and the memory of his touch from so long ago lingers in the center of my cells.

A shuffle at my bedroom door causes me to look up. *Pa.*

"Your ma saw you fall into a heap that afternoon. The one where you'd caught the bus to Thomas's school. She hated so much that love had led to her daughter's shattered heart, she'd wanted to drive out to the Abads' and demand an answer . . . anything from them and the young Thomas."

"Why didn't she?" I twirl the cup in my hand.

"Because I stopped her, Spooky. I reminded her that true love was never a simple or easy journey."

———

THE DRIVE HOME to Simon's Town is shorter today than it is most days. That's Sunday traffic for you. The sun sits high in the midday sky, its radiance bleaching the blue from the heavens. My stomach gurgles. I'm hungry. I decide its time I pull up my big-girl undies and get me something sweet. My stomach feels stronger, and some gelato would do it good.

I pull into a lucky opening right in front of the little ice crème vendor. The area is packed with locals and visitors enjoying the sunshine and water.

Double honey crunch with caramel, yum! Much better than coffee and toast, which was my plan for a late lunch.

The same odd feeling from the other day tickles my nerve endings.

"Enough already!"

"Uh sorry, *Sissi*?" The young man behind the counter gives me a startled glance.

"Agh, sorry. I was thinking out loud," I say and hand him a twenty rand and place my order.

No more weird stories of how awesome love is, or bonded souls, or fate. So I kissed a boy fourteen years ago and it didn't work out. Many girls' first kisses don't work out.

. . . Hasten home for it be time for your heart ta show da way . . .

I ignore the voice in my head as I turn to take in the beautiful summer surroundings, and my eyes fall on a familiar, tall muscled frame.

———

Thomas rose from his seat beneath the old fig tree. He'd gone there after spending another morning unpacking boxes and dusting off photo albums in the storage unit. He'd needed to find peace and let go of his anger and hurt. He'd instantly noticed Rochelle, with her blonde faerie-colored locks falling down her back, as she'd jumped out of the white double cab.

He watched as she pointed to the list of toppings and ordered her treat. He loved how her face lit up with the anticipation of digging into the frozen dessert. Not even a child enjoyed ice crème as much as this woman seemed to. He clenched his fists and gritted his teeth. How was it a battle-ready naval lieutenant was afraid of speaking to her?

Thomas had seen action before he became an instructor, but even that did not compare to the fear and apprehension running rampant inside him as he made his way to where Rochelle stood.

The sea was calm after the windy weekend. It reminded him of her eyes. Sweat trickled down his neck and back, and his stomach imitated jumping beans.

Then she turned and saw him.

He placed one nervous sandal-clad foot in front of the other and crossed the short distance between them.

Now or never.

"Hello, Rochelle."

He noted her body stiffening. Her eyes were wide, her cheeks flushed.

"Here we go," the vendor called out behind her.

She turned. "Thank you." She reached for her ice crème. Holding it in her hand, she cocked her head and squinted her eyes. "Hello, Thomas." Her voice was smooth and exactly as he remembered it from all those years ago.

"I . . . I just want to . . ." *Bliksem!* Why wouldn't his words come out?

She cocked her head and shoved a hand in her jean-short pockets.

"Can we sit?" Thomas pointed to the bench beneath the tree.

She looked past him. Her eyes flooded with emotion as her lips straightened and the natural flush on her cheeks deepened. Okay, what now?

"Look, I can't just ignore you every time we . . . It's a small town; we're bound to run into one another."

Rochelle straightened her back and head, the way women do when they want to make a point. "It was easy enough to pretend I didn't exist fourteen years ago."

He deserved that. Her words, her anger, her pain. But like a gut punch, it knocked the wind out of him. He stood, gaping like a guppy fish, as she ordered a second cone.

Thanking the vendor, she pushed the cone into Thomas's hand and walked away. But she didn't head for her car. Instead she headed for the bench beneath the tree and sat down, turning her bright turquoise gaze onto him.

Like a hummingbird to a *suikerbos*, Thomas followed. His heart beat harder than when he'd run the Comrades last year. Was she giving him a second chance? Not at love, but perhaps, at forgiveness? Was it a good sign she'd bought him an ice crème too?

8
———

A SLIGHT BREEZE PICKS UP AND ON IT RIDE THE WORDS which have haunted me since the day the old woman came to see me.

"There be a time for all tha things in dis world...

Shhhh . . . I tell my heart. *The fig tree is a coincidence. So is running into Thomas.*

I taste the lie in my thoughts as they make their way to my mouth, and I swallow them. Instead I turn to look at the man following me to the bench beneath the branches of wisdom.

I want to rant. I want to throw my arms around his neck, and I want to throw a three-year-old tantrum. But I know this is not the way to handle the emotions I've ignored for the last fourteen years.

He's right. This is a small town and chances are, we'd run into one another again. I'm not going to forgo my ice crème forever. Best we face the past together and sort it out once and for all.

I'm as confused as a Zebra without stripes. My heart screams for more of him, but my head warns me of the hurt I almost didn't survive the time before. I had to work my soul into oblivion last week so I could try not to feel what I'm feeling right now. Thomas has gnawed away at my conscience.

I don't like the way my insides melt as he sits beside me. His large brown eyes and beautiful open face, with the scar above his left eye, call to me. My finger aches to trace it. My lips burn . . . *No, no, no!*

We sit in silence and eat our gelato.

I try not to stare at the way his tongue licks his rainbow delight sitting cozily inside the waffle cone. I wish that was me.

No!

With our frozen desserts finished, we turn to face one another. Thomas fidgets with his serviette, and I sit on my hands to try and camouflage my nerves.

"Well?" I hope I sound cocky enough.

"I owe you an apology."

"Yes, you do." I try not to sound too bitchy, but it's hard. So many emotions I refused to deal with in the past are returning to haunt me.

"Y-yes. What I did back then . . . it was . . . was..."

I stand and pace in front of the bench. I'm not sure how to handle this. I think I owe him an apology too.

"I'm also sorry. The other day . . . I didn't expect to see you after all this time."

"I understand. Believe me." A soft, knowing smile opens up his face, and all I want to do is cup it in my hands and kiss him.

No!

A weird silence surrounds us. Is that it? My heart begs as the sixteen-year-old Rochelle demands a declaration of love.

I round on him. "Is that all?"

Thomas stands, and I stop pacing. His body is a hand's breadth from me. I look up. His brown eyes melt into a hot gold.

"I was a sixteen-year-old boy who'd been told his entire life what a burden I was to my family. So when my uncle threatened to disown me, throw me out onto the street, after beating the nonsense out of me first, I knew I had to obey. I had to protect you from his wrath too."

What? "I thought you . . ."

He places his large, strong hands on my shoulders, and my knees buckle.

We sit. His hands slide from my shoulders into my palms, which lay quivering on my lap. Flashes of my romantic dreams invade my common sense and heat pools between my thighs. Good grief! Could my body please grow up? I'm almost thirty. Surely, I can control my emotions and my attraction.

"Rochelle, what we shared that night was a once-in-a-lifetime moment. But we were young, and life was hard for me. How could I be anything if all my uncle told me was how useless I was? How my mother had shamed them. How I was proof of her shame. Who did I think I was, carrying on with a white girl, of all things? I won't even mention the empty bottle of wine."

Shame and years of pain contort his features, and he looks away. Suddenly, everything makes sense. The returned letters. The unanswered messages. His ignoring me. He was frightened, more for me than himself.

I reach up to stroke his cheek, but the sentiment feels too intimate, so I pull my hand away. "Look at me."

He turns his head.

"I'm sorry. I should have known better."

"How could you. We were both so young, so innocent, and my damned uncle..."

———

WE SPEND the rest of the day catching up and walking beside the water. My anger and fear have waned. It's so easy to be in this man's company.

"Losing Mom was almost as bad as managing a broken heart," I say as we stroll along the quay. "Sorry." I remember that mine wasn't the only broken heart.

"What was it like moving to a new country?" he asks.

"Fun, scary, exciting, scary . . ." I chuckle, and his gaze turns to molten lava.

I look away before I do something I might regret, like kiss him. I want to reach up and taste his lips on mine so badly.

Instead, I regale him with stories of my time working for Doctors Without Borders.

"The first time I arrived in Sierra Leone was an eye opener. South Africa is dangerous if one isn't street-smart, but North Africa is a whole other ball game. I almost wet my pants the first time our clinic was robbed by a local militia. After that, we learned to bury most of our meds and only leave out enough for them not to think we were hiding anything. And don't get me started on the reporters. They pretend they're all 'I'm here to show the world the truth' but in reality, they twist every bit of it."

"Why?" He frowns, and I bite back the urge to wrap my arms around his neck and forget about the world and the last fourteen years.

"Because it's always about reaching prime-time news and hiding the fact that most of the money chari-ties raise for the poor, at no time reaches them; it's never about the truth!" I don't mean to, but the anger I have for mainstream media and their manipulative storytelling has me fisting my hands.

"So, you believe in the fake news phenomena?"

"It's not a phenomenon. It's alive and deadly, and half of the planet follows it like brain-dead zombies." I realize I'm getting too worked up and stop to take a deep breath.

"Why, Doctor, aren't zombies already brain-dead?" He teases, and we both burst out laughing.

"Sorry."

Thomas stops and considers me. "Don't be. It's so good to laugh and hear you laugh." Thomas reaches up and strokes my cheek with his thumb.

He leans toward me just as a loud male voice shouts, "Duck!" And a rugby ball comes whizzing past our heads.

"Sorry, *bras*." The young guy trots by in his swimmers and a baseball cap, leans down and grabs the ball, then jogs off with his mates.

Thomas waves. "All good." He shakes his head.

We continue our stroll from the beach up onto the boardwalk. Above our heads a seagull calls, and life, for the moment, is almost sublime.

"Why'd you do it if it was so dangerous?"

Thomas asks a question I've never considered. Why did I sign up for a job which paid little to nothing and had my life balancing on a tightrope every moment of every day? But it's not an answer which requires contemplation.

"Because I'm a doctor, and these people haven't seen decent health care at any point in their lives. Every human being deserves someone who gives a damn about them. There are too many who are out to stomp on the weak for their own gain." I try to smile as

I push away the darker memories. The time when our head doctor was taken for ransom and returned in bits and pieces. Or the domestic violence and child abuse which runs rife amongst those communities.

"And because it irritates me how rich, spoiled brats protest for human rights, but don't know a damn thing about what really goes on. People who don't know should leave it to us that do, or be willing to get their hands dirty. I wanted to know, to make a difference and I think in some small way, I did. "

"What is it that is really going on? I mean what did you see for yourself?" Thomas's sincerity causes me to take pause.

"I sound like all the loud mouths on social media but the news lies. Mainstream media is preventing the whole, unedited truth to be shown. Everything is twisted to follow a path which serves those who lust for power. The bullshit rhetoric the media and ass-hat social media spread and that is then picked up by ignorant keyboard warriors who've never left the comfort of their couches and take it upon themselves to judge and finger point. People need to be educated. What's the easiest way to bring a culture or a country to its knees? Destroy the education system and feed them conspiracies, lies, and superstitions. To take away humanity's freedom of choice and ability to think for ourselves." I stop and roll my head back to ease the tension in my neck.

This shit makes me so mad.

"The world knows nothing, and there are days when all I want to do is slap ignorant twitterers upside their heads!"

"Is that what you did. Healed and educated?"

"Yeah, where I could . . . where *we* could. It takes a team effort. But there were days where we fought never-ending uphill battles."

"I know you made a difference." Thomas's expression shows a belief in me I've never had in myself, and it almost brings me to tears.

"But that's enough about that. What's the Navy like?"

Thomas entertains me with stories of cheeky sailors and his time at sea. "Agh, we had this one *poophol*. Poor guy never caught a lucky break in his life. Not until he joined the Navy. We're out to sea. I can't tell you where or why . . ."

"Or you'd have to kill me?" I throw the overused cliché at him and add my most flirtatious smile.

Thomas throws his head back, and the sultriest laughter fills my ears.

When we've both recovered, he scoffs, "Miss Le Roux, you best tread carefully, or I may have to throw you in the brig."

I reply with only a flutter of eyelashes, not mentioning what I think I can do with a pair of handcuffs and those bars.

"I was sad to hear about your mom." He gives me a sympathetic smile.

"It's life. Pa's never been the same since . . ." I sigh and look out over the water. It's calm, and the rhythmic ebb and flow of the cerulean waves soothe my nerves. "What happened to your folks?"

He turns to face the ocean just as I have, folding his hands behind his back, like a sailor standing at ease. I dare a glance. His face is so handsome. Clean-shaven, smooth olive skin, titian hair drinking in the summer sun. I want to run my fingers through the short wavy strands. I ache for him to pull me into those ripped arms, bulging from beneath his white polo shirt. For him to kiss me and make me his. Some part of me knows he does too. I can see it in his eyes. But neither of us dare. The hurt is still fresh in our hearts.

"They were killed in a car hijacking when I was three. I don't remember much." His smile is sad. "I received a letter a few days ago. And a phone call . . . from your pa." He pauses.

I swallow. So that was what Pa was hiding. "Oh."

"*Ja.* Seems he knew my dad very well."

"Oh." Well I knew that part, but the revelation still catches me off guard.

"He's a good man, your pa. He's made sure I'll finally find out all about my mom and dad."

"Oh."

I'm a broken record, but it's all I can muster as the sensual aura of romance evaporates and is replaced with my growing confabulation. Pa had said he knew

Thomas's parents, but mentioned nothing about making contact with him.

Thomas sighs then explains, "Don't be angry with him. He obviously had his reasons."

I feign a smile.

"My parents left me a small inheritance and a storeroom filled with photo albums, books, and journals all about them. My mom was a brilliant history scholar who married my dad, a second-generation South African Scotsman. And, reading his diary, it was clear he was absolutely besotted with her. Until their murder, I got to travel through Africa with them. If I close my eyes and try real hard, I can almost see their faces smiling down at me."

"What did your father do? Was he also into history?" I don't mention Pa has already told me he was a cop. I don't want Thomas thinking we discussed any of his business behind his back.

"Of a sort. Seemed he worked for some international police force—Interpol. I think he investigated stolen art but then, I haven't finished reading his diary. He happened upon a ring of human traffickers. The case somehow intertwined with stolen artifacts from Egypt and other North African countries. Strangely his discoveries are as relevant today as they were twenty-seven years ago." His voice trails off as I watch his mind chew on what he's just told me.

My mind piques at the mention of the words "human" and "trafficking," but I contain myself as I see him swallow back his grief. The love he was robbed of is carved into the sides of his mouth.

I fight the urge to wrap my arms around him, to soak up some of the pain so evident on his face. The attraction between us is still there. It never died or vanished, but I can't let him back in. I can't ever hurt like that again. There are too many barriers between us, the biggest being his faith and our differing heritages. He'd never say that to my face. But I know, as all South Africans do, mixed relationships are still frowned upon.

Instead, I rest a hand on his shoulder. "Sorry."

"It's okay," he whispers.

A sharp beeping sound disturbs the moment.

"I have to go." He fidgets with his watch. "I must get back to base. I come here most days for lunch. Perhaps I'll see you?"

"Yes, perhaps." I smile, trying to act brave, but his close proximity sends blood rushing like a stormy ocean through my head. I ignore the dizzy sensation.

He leans forward, and my heart jumps in my throat. I close my eyes and my lips tingle in anticipation. But, he touch my forehead, and my heart crashes into my toes. Why had I hoped for more? This is the best for the both of us, isn't it?

I watch him walk away, leaving only emptiness and confusion to accompany me home.

———

"WHAT HAPPENED?" Pa asks, as I lay the table for three. Raymond's gone to wash his hands. I wish I could figure out what that no-good scoundrel is up to.

"With what?" I ask, knowing perfectly well what Pa means, but I don't want Raymond to hear.

Pa gives me an impatient huff. It's Wednesday evening and time for our weekly meal together.

"We spoke. He mentioned you and your *skelm* phone call to him. We caught up, and that's about it. I don't think he sees me as anything more than a friend. Not that I want to be anything more than that," I lie.

"Be patient, Spooky. These things take time, and it must be hard for him."

"Why didn't you tell me?" I can no longer hide my frustration.

"It is not my story to tell, Spook. He will tell you when he's ready. Seems he's already started to." Pa smiles.

"What story?" Raymond struts into the kitchen.

"Nothing," I mumble and slam the last fork down on the placemat.

"Give anything else to the second-born?" Raymond's accusation riles me.

Pa shakes his head but says nothing else. I try and do the same. What in the seven heavens is Raymond after? Because I know it's not only the cup.

"What are you doing here?" I sound far more snappish than I mean to.

"Agh, relax, Sis. It's my home too you know. I wanted to soak up some of the good family vibes."

Heat invades my cheeks, but I don't give Raymond the satisfaction he seeks. Instead I answer with a cold silence. I know he's lying. Two visits in one week? I doubt it very much.

"What? You think because you finished school and gave so much of yourself to the poor that you're Pa's favorite now?"

I watch as he sits and pours himself wine, not offering to pour for either Pa or myself. A leopard truly does not change its spots, and Raymond Le Roux is up to no good.

"Got a job?" I ask.

"What's it to you?" he all but spits.

"Now, now, you two. Let's eat and try to behave like a decent family. For Ma?" Pa's words hit home. Even Raymond quietens down. He was a good brother until Ma got sick. And his true colors appeared almost overnight.

9

When Thomas wasn't teaching, or sitting on the planning exercises being run to combat the latest terror on the high seas, he used every spare moment to work through the storage unit in the industrial park just outside of Cape Town. He was amazed at how well the books, furniture, and other things had remained over twenty-six years.

He sat on the cold, concrete floor, staring down at a photo of his three-year-old self, his beautiful mom, whose eyes he'd inherited, and his broad shouldered, auburn-haired father, when his phone rang.

It was *Oom* Derrek. "How are things going, my boy?"

"Fine thanks, *Oom*. I'm actually in the storage room as we speak," Thomas greeted, using the Afrikaans form of address which carried the greatest respect.

Unlike in English, one never called their elder Mr. or Sir, but *oom*.

"Oh, that's good. Have you had time to go over to the house?"

"I was thinking I'd do that tomorrow perhaps . . . It's just . . . it's all so much to take in." Thomas tried to keep the sadness from his voice.

"Ja, I understand. It can't be easy. Look, when you are more settled, come around for a visit. I have one last item to give you. It's important. It was your father's. You will know what to do with it."

Derrek would not elaborate over the phone and his tone caused every instinct in Thomas's Navy-honed body to rise.

———

THOMAS DROVE BACK to the base from the storage units. His mind tripped over all he'd discovered.

The house his parents had owned was located in Fish Hoek. He'd only spent five minutes looking around it the first time he'd gone. It'd been hard to imagine the home had once been filled with his childish laughter and the love of his parents. He left after he saw the doorpost of what must have been his bedroom, marked with two black lines, the date, and his height. But he couldn't avoid the past forever. Tomorrow he would drive out and take another look.

Ibrahim's hateful, greedy nature had cost him so much.

It was late afternoon, and the sun was sinking into the ocean. Its soft reds and magentas streaked across the sky like heaven's breath. Thomas looked back at the road. He was not heading for the naval base but driving toward the ice crème vendor.

Dammit!

He flicked the indicator to turn around when he spotted Rochelle.

He should go. What was he doing here? Instead of concentrating, he'd lost himself in thought and his heart's desire had brought him to this location. For reasons beyond his comprehension, he flicked off his indicator, drove on, parked in front of the small gelato vendor, turned off the engine, and got out.

"Hi." She smiled, wiping her mouth with the serviette. "Want one?" She pointed a thumb over her shoulder toward the vendor.

Few women enjoyed tasty treats these days. They were all too worried about their weight. But Rochelle was different. She found joy in her small frozen delight.

"Do you have to rush back?" He had a sudden urge to share the week's events with her. Strange how comfortable he felt in her company. Stranger still how his heart had brought him back here.

"I've just finished a shift. Hectic day. But why don't you come over for supper?"

———

O.M.G! Have I honestly invited him over to my place for dinner? What in God's name has possessed me? And I can't even cook!

"That'd be great. I don't have to clock-in at the base until tomorrow."

My heart leaps as his smile stretches across his beautiful face. A dimple makes itself known on the cleft of his chin. Few men smile the way Thomas does: open, beautiful, unafraid of the world.

Calm down, Rochelle. It's only dinner between friends.

"Okay, do you eat Chinese?" I ask.

"You know how to cook Asian food?"

"Ah, no. But I do know how to order in." I hope that doesn't put him off.

His smile broadens. "Great, as long as it's from Won Ton down the road. They have the best pork dumplings."

"Totally. Um, I'll drive with you. My apartment is around the corner. I walk to work." I point in the direction of a block of flats peeking over the top of the hospital building sitting behind some holiday apartments across the road.

"*Ja*, sure! Geez you're lucky to have found a place so close to work. This area is all rentals for holidaymakers."

"*Ja*, no, I tell you, it was pure luck. I was the one who put stitches in the son of the agent who runs the rentals for that block." I give him another cheeky grin. "Shall we go?" I wave toward his car.

His eyes turn from warm to sultry, and again I remind myself this is simply dinner with a friend.

———

"It was the strangest sensation reading that letter. I'd never thought of myself as the beloved child of anyone. But there it stood in black on faded white paper. My mother and father treasured me and left me all their worldly possessions so that I may not only remember them, but never forget how much they loved me." Thomas's voice breaks on the last word, and I swallow a mouthful of honey chicken and tears.

"You said they'd left photo albums too."

Thomas shifts in his seat as he looks past me and the window at my back.

"She was so beautiful." His voice is soft but riddled with a mixture of love, despair, and wonder. "I look a lot like her . . . I think. And my dad. He was a big man. Mom wrote in one of her diaries how he had Viking genes in his blood."

I blink away the tears burning the back of my eyes as Thomas returns his gaze to me.

I place my empty container on the coffee table beside me. Downing the last sip of my soda I look at Thomas sitting opposite me on the couch. "Wow, that's intense. And your Uncle?" I want to know more and hope I'm not pushing the boundaries of our newly forged friendship.

"He's lied to me all my life. He never cared for me. I have a feeling, and I know this sounds out there . . ." He swallows hard. "But I think the only reason I survived all those years was because of the inheritance."

"But why? What is it to him? He's probably one of the richest blokes in Simon's Town!" I struggle to digest Thomas revelations.

"I'm not sure. But I'm going to find out."

"Just be careful. Pa's warned me about him . . . Sorry, I know he's your uncle." I really need to think before I say things.

"Don't be. There's no love lost between us. He really is a good man, you know."

"Who?"

"Your pa. He did so much for me, and he regrets never being able to save me from Ibrahim. But I made sure that he knows I don't blame him for it."

I suck in a breath as Thomas's revelation knocks me for a six.

"You didn't know?" Thomas asks.

I shake my head. No wonder Pa asked my forgiveness. After our last chat, I had an inkling there was more to his involvement, but not to the extent Thomas has revealed. But I'm not angry, simply shocked.

"Was it that bad?" I need to know.

Thomas drops his head and his shoulders sag. For a while we sit in silence before he straightens and looks at me. I try not to lose myself in his hot chocolate gaze.

"I was a nuisance to Ibrahim. A reminder of his defiant younger sister and the white man she'd married. Until I met you, I'd forgotten what it was to be looked at with wonderment . . ." He swallows his words as he wipes a hand down his face. ". . . instead of hatred and disgust. My childhood was a series of lessons which consisted of standing out in the cold until it pleased Ibrahim, and days locked up in a closet in the passage."

I want to fling my arms around this brave man and tell him that he's safe now. But I swallow my tears and change the subject. "Pa did mention he knew your parents."

Thomas smiles. "Yeah. I must say it's all thrown me a bit. Um, listen, if you're not working tomorrow after-noon, would you come to my home with me?" His request is the cherry on top of all the surprises I've been served this afternoon.

"To your parents' house?" Oh, wow, this is huge. Too huge. Perhaps I . . . I stand and walk over to the balcony of my small home. The sun has set and a sea breeze has picked up, and I close my eyes and allow it to wash over me. I turn and walk back.

Thomas hasn't taken his gaze off of me, and the dimple reappears as I sit down beside him and melt.

"*Ja.* I understand if you're working or it's too much." Thomas shifts uncomfortably.

The impulsive silliness from this afternoon takes over my brain again. I simply can't help myself when I am around this man. I place my hand on his. Fire and ice invade every cell of my body. "I'd be honored to."

As. A. Friend.

I'm supporting him as a friend. I can't get close to this man. I'll ruin it. Forget that he turns my insides into mush—we're only friends.

Thomas helps me clear the leftover containers and, as I rinse out our glasses, he strolls over to the open balcony doors. We've had soda, but now I need something a little stronger. I am not sure if I should offer him wine or not.

"Did you keep this?" I turn and find Thomas standing in my lounge with the pewter cup Pa gave me in his hands.

My insides flip. I'd left it on the sideboard after unpacking the other afternoon.

"Uh, no, yes . . . well, it's a long story."

"Tell me?" He smiles.

"Look, I must ask, and only because I won't feel comfortable drinking if you can't."

He squints at my weird explanation.

"Do you drink, or . . .?"

He throws his head back and laughs. It's that beautiful hearty sound from the day we walked on the beach, one which begs a person to join in. "Sorry. I'm not laughing at you, it's just after everything . . . Yes, I drink. No, I don't practice my uncle's religion. I haven't, not since I left school and joined the Navy. In fact, I don't practice any religion."

"Oh good. I mean . . . ugh . . . How's a white?"

He nods, and I open the fridge.

"Cape Point Sav Blanc?" I call to him.

"I didn't think wine farmers drank wine they hadn't produced themselves?"

I jump. I hadn't heard him follow me into the kitchen.

"Sorry, I didn't mean to . . ." Thomas steps toward me as I twist around and come face-to-face with the man who's haunted my sleep these last months.

With a finger, he tucks a strand of wayward hair behind my ear, setting my skin on fire as he moves forward. His eyes pin me to the spot.

Everything stops. Time. My heart. My thoughts.

He leans into me as his hand slides around my waist and presses against the hollow of my back, and he lowers his head.

His lips are warm, and soft as silk. Wisps of spice, the kind only a man can exude, push away my fear. I let go of the fridge door and allow my hands to glide up beneath his T-shirt and over the lush skin of his torso. My fingertips ride the bulges and valleys of his toned abs and chest. He is built like a warrior. Solid. Strong.

I want him. I need him. I . . .

I slide my hands up and cup the back of his neck and pull him closer as our kiss intensifies.

Stop!

My fear pushes back. I pull away.

Thomas relaxes his embrace.

"I missed you." It's all he says, before he lets me go. "Where are your wine glasses?"

It takes me a moment to catch up with what's just happened. "Uh—um—top right-hand cupboard, above the sink."

What. The. Hell?

10

Every last atom in his body exploded in a shower of sparks and lightning as he placed his lips on hers. The release of years of restrained emotions threatened to overtake the need to take it slowly. He willed his fingers not to undress her, but instead to linger over the soft skin of her neck, as he fought back the need to taste every inch of her. Raw desire begged him to pick her up and carry her to bed. To offer himself to her. He wanted to be hers, forever, and he wanted to make her his.

But not yet.

Thomas had yearned for Rochelle's lips the way parched earth longed for rain. Like the desert sands, his soul soaked in the touch of her velvet mouth and the sweetness it promised to deliver. He'd stuffed up the last time they were together; he wasn't about to forego the chance again.

He simply couldn't help himself. The way every word fell from her lips with meaning, filled with substance. The sensuous flutter of her eyelids and the way her gaze held his. Her sincerity when she listened to him as he told her about his parents and the photos and Ibrahim.

It was the way she walked to the kitchen, the sway of her hips, the smell of sweet candied heaven hugging her like the mist hugged the berg. It was everything she was, washing away his last vestiges of resistance. He simply had to taste her.

She'd wanted him too. He saw it, tasted it, felt it . . . and then she'd pushed him away.

No matter. He knew he'd have to take it slow. Like him, she was still coming to terms with that night sixteen years ago and her Pa's involvement in Thomas's current situation.

Thomas held his breath to calm his galloping heart, then exhaled slowly as he poured the wine.

He knew this brand well. With its fresh peach and raw hazelnut flavor, the makers did it justice by blending it with a Semillon. He handed her a glass.

Her eyes were bright like twinkling stars and her lips plump from their kiss. He needed to steer them both away from the canyon of emotions settling in the quiet between them.

"So, what's the long story?" He grabbed the cup from the counter before following her to the couch and sitting. Leaning forward, he placed the cup on the coffee table then took a long sip from his wine.

Rochelle eyed him. Her right eyebrow cocked ever so slightly. She was processing. She sipped her wine. He felt his eyes drawn to her lips as they hugged the rim of the glass.

"Agh, it's an old wives' tale passed down from generation to generation with the silly thing." She paused as if to judge his reaction.

"Go on." His insides twisted as she licked her lips.

No more kissing!

"Okay." She shifted her body away from him, creating a cold, lonely chasm.

"The cup was part of a set of twelve, made in the early fifteen-hundreds, as a wedding gift to some distant relative of mine in France." She stopped and took a deep glug of wine. "But along the way, many got stolen or lost and only this one remained. Stories were passed on from generation to generation about its origins and soon, it was believed the cup held a charm." She looked at the cup, then to Thomas.

"Is it a lucky cup?" he asked.

"Ha! Pa would love for me to think so. He says it brings together those hearts who were meant to be."

Thomas felt his cheeks redden as he focused on the inscription. "And this?"

"It's French. Reads something along the lines of, *Wine is proof that God loves us and loves to see us happy.*"

The words pulled Thomas back to that night fourteen years ago. He remembered the cake, the singing, the sulking, sweet, sixteen-year-old Rochelle.

"I don't believe in luck, curses, or visions," she says as though to tell herself more than him.

"Visions?" He had to ask.

Rochelle downed her wine then reached for the bottle and poured another glass, before topping his up. "A medicine woman approached me before I came home from Sierra Leone."

"Oh . . . as in a *sangoma*?"

"You could liken them, yes."

"Why?" He placed the cup down and reached for his own wine, sipped, and waited for her to reply. The look on her face told him she was still struggling with whatever had happened in North Africa.

"You don't have to tell me." He placed a hand on hers where it rested on her knee. The hair on his arms stood upright followed by a rush of goosebumps.

"Agh, it's a load of rubbish. She basically told me I would regret not returning home. That there was a shadow hanging over my pa, and that my one true love waited for me beneath the arms of wisdom."

Every muscle in his body stiffened and his breath hitched in his throat. Some part of this story, however outlandish, rang true.

"Look, I am not making any of this up because . . . because of what happened there." She pointed to the kitchen. Her cheeks reddened, reminding Thomas of strawberry lollipops.

"Or what happened fourteen years ago?" Thomas took a deep sip of his own wine. Had he complicated the situation by not curbing his need?

His lips ached to taste more of her. He wanted to kiss her again. Kiss the dimple on her left cheek, then kiss his way down her neck and . . . *stop!*

"Pa reckons there are souls who were meant to be together forever."

"As in, you and me?" While Derrek had been nothing but great these last few days over the phone, Thomas had always imagined him to be against their romantic interlude.

"Yes." Rochelle sipped her wine, not looking at him. Thomas didn't miss the slight tremor of her hand.

"But . . . I always thought . . . weren't he and your mother against us? The same way my uncle and aunt were?" He fumbled for the right words as the revelation sank in.

"No. Funnily enough, Pa has done nothing but mention you and your whereabouts in every conversation we've had since I've returned."

Thomas leaned back into the couch. "Why? Because he knew my parents?"

"No."

He noticed a soft blush color her cheeks and neck.

"He actually wanted to see us together?" The epiphany conjured a soft hint of excitement in side of him.

"You don't seem weirded out by all this?" Rochelle tucked a leg beneath her bum.

Thomas placed his glass down, then turned. He was about to rest both his hands on her legs, then decided not to. If he touched her now, he'd ask for another kiss.

Perhaps, if they dealt with what happened all those years ago, it would help in taming his desires. Or even help her get over her fear and stop her from pushing him away. He knew their attraction was mutual. A blind man would be able to sense the chemistry between them.

But that something in her heart which held her back could only be the rejection of that night fourteen years ago.

He focused on her face, as his periphery vision caught the rise and fall of her bosom, the darkening of her lips, the dilation of her pupils. His blood raced through his body as his heart beat to the staccato tempo of a lone drum.

"What do you remember about that night, your birthday, when we kissed?"

"That your uncle hates me, that he and your auntie believe I lured you into the devil's den, and that it was a fat mess."

"No, forget that. Forget him. Try to remember beyond the pain and embarrassment." Thomas waved his hands in the air, trying hard to ignore the need to slide them up her legs, grip her ass, and pull her onto him.

Their eyes met, and an electric ozone brewed in the air.

His palms burned to run along her bare skin. To pull off her T-shirt and fill his mouth with her ample breasts. Instead he buried his urges and picked his glass up again, but perhaps more wine wasn't such a good idea? He needed a distraction, like yesterday!

"Do you remember how we were drawn to each other that night? While the grown-ups were arguing issues beyond our interests?"

Rochelle nodded. "Yes, it was as though there was a cord attached between us, pulling one toward the other."

"Exactly. And when we poured the wine . . ."

"The stars, the crickets . . . the world turned her focus on us and forgot everyone else."

"I remember it as though it were last night." Thomas said.

"Why are you asking me to remember this?"

"Because I want you to see that it wasn't all about the hurt."

The soft turquoise in Rochelle's gaze deepened to a mystic blue as she pulled her hands through her hair again.

The movement wafted her candy floss scent in his direction. He didn't do sweet, but this woman made him drool for sugar. Her caramel aroma intoxicated his better judgement. Thomas fought the need to fist her hair and pull her mouth to his.

No!

Thomas stood and walked out onto the balcony. Fresh air and the cool ocean breeze were what he needed.

Her voice followed him. "I clung to the good memories for a long time, even after you ignored me that day outside your school gates."

"I should have tried harder." Thomas couldn't feign the note of regret in his voice.

"As you said, we were kids, Thomas, and your uncle . . . Pa said he'd done terrible things to you."

Thomas cringed inwardly. Then he realized that what he'd heard in her last comment was understanding.

Rochelle came to stand beside him. Her finger reached up and traced the scar on his forehead. "You can tell me. I can't take away the hurt, but I can share the burden."

Her words almost buckled Thomas's knees. No one had ever cared enough to ask.

"It was the day of my matric graduation when I told Ibrahim I would not devote my life to his religion. It was also the last time he ever laid a hand on me." Thomas raised his hand and traced the furrow of damaged tissue where Rochelle's fingers had skimmed seconds earlier.

Her eyes brimmed with tears. "I wish I could wash

away all those years of abuse and hurt." Her voice trembled.

"I don't need your pity."

She flinched.

He had no idea how to deal with empathy when it came to the years of pain he'd suffered by the hand of Ibrahim Abad. "Sorry. It was a painful time. One that hurts to remember."

Her eyes shone with understanding and a love he'd never dreamed he'd ever be worthy of.

"We may have been apart these last fourteen years, but I've never connected with any other woman the way I do with you."

His bold words caused her to step back.

She's not within your reach, Thomas. The old voice of doubt echoed across his soul.

Bugger his doubt and bugger his uncle.

"It is not your burden to bear." He pulled her into him and wrapped his arms around her. "But thank you for giving a damn when no one else has."

He was carried away on a magic carpet. Floating between the stars. His hand cupped her neck. Her skin, so soft and warm, so inviting. His hand slipped higher, her hair like silk, his fingers curling around her locks.

"Thomas . . ." she said as one hand balled his shirt and pulled him closer, and her other pushed him away.

11

HOLY HELL!

There were no words, only emotions. Raw, hungry, sizzling-hot, sticky, mucky emotions. How was he going to keep his distance when all he wanted to do was make her his? When all he needed was Rochelle Le Roux in every possible way? Now, tomorrow, forever.

The Navy taught a person many life skills, but they sure as shit had no manual or training code on how to negotiate one's desires or heart.

Thomas leaned back against the cool metallic wall of the elevator as it floated down to the ground floor of the apartment block. Why had fate brought her back into his life when he could not have her? It was clear by their awkward embrace she was not comfortable with his advances.

Yet the way she'd responded to his kiss before she'd

pushed him away told him all he needed to know. She wanted him as much as he wanted her. He'd not pushed her. She needed more time than him, and he'd give her another fourteen years if that was what it took.

What if he ended up hurting her as he had all those years ago? Perhaps the safest path was to remain friends?

No, he would prove his worth. He'd never hurt her again.

Tomorrow would be a test of their newfound path together. He'd simply have to resist any more advances. It would be hard. When he was around that woman, his every decent intention fled.

The elevator pinged, and the doors opened. The foyer wasn't lit well, and the entrance stood at an angle, so it made it easy for Thomas to spot the man standing across the road. A built-in alarm, which he'd come to trust, shot a jolt of electricity into his diaphragm.

Something about the stranger was out of place. The man was tall, with light hair, difficult to see if it were blond or light brown in the off-orange streetlight. There was a vague familiarity about his face. But Thomas was sure they'd never met.

Thomas stepped back into the shadows of the foyer and watched as the man finished his cigarette, then dropped the butt on the ground before walking off. That was when Thomas made his way to his car, instinctively bracing for an attack, and grateful for the electric security gates keeping any trespassers out and away from Rochelle.

This bloke was definitely scoping out the joint. He should warn Rochelle.

No, there was no need to alarm her.

Instead, he pulled his phone from his pocket and SMSed a buddy in the police force. Best have it checked out. If the bloke saw more police activity around the place, he might back off.

Thomas gave the street a thorough once-over and climbed into his car. He pulled out of the parking spot and glanced into his rearview mirror. The stranger hadn't returned. Good.

Back in his room at the barracks, Thomas dove into the pile of diaries he'd brought back from the storage unit.

One with a soft, bronze silk cover had the name *Kasih Campbell* embroidered across it, and it called to him.

He surfed the Net for the locations his mother mentioned in her notes. These were all places he'd travelled to with her and his father as a child. Some exotic, others war-torn and desolate. One in particular, she'd circled in bright red. A city off the coast of Cameroon by the name of Douala. But it was the words written in red beside the circled name which caused Thomas's heckles to rise.

Stolen Benin Artifacts shipped with children. Must show Henry.

Thomas took a screen shot of the page and sent *Oom* Derrek a message.

Can I come by tomorrow afternoon?

It was after ten, and he hoped he hadn't disturbed the older man. He should have waited until morning, but everything about this seemed to scream urgency.

His phone rang.

"Sorry I bothered you so late, *Oom*," Thomas apologized as he answered.

"No need, my boy. I'd have replied to your message except I'm a little *dof* where technology is concerned. Rochelle's spent the last month trying to get me to use that 'What's' something or another to video chat on, anyway. Yes, do come over tomorrow. I have some work to finish, so the late afternoon will probably be better."

"That's great, *Oom*. Thanks."

Arrangements were finalized to meet at Nooitgedacht the following day.

Thomas would pick Rochelle up after work. They'd go to the house and then to the farm.

"Who else knows about this?" Derrek's voice carried a warning which caused Thomas's insides to freeze.

"Only me and you. Rochelle knows I've been reading Mom's diaries. Why?"

"Keep it hushed, my boy. No one else needs to know."

So, there was something important about this.

"Alright, *oom*. See you tomorrow. *Lekka slaap*." He

wished the *oom* a good night's rest. His instincts, as always, were on point. Did all of this link up with whatever it was *Oom* Derrek had of his father's?

————

THE COOL SHOWER does nothing to calm my rampaging hormones or temper my anxiety. If I wasn't such a realist, I swear I'd believe the insane notion brewing in my mind. That what I feel is twofold: his and mine, ours—our insecurity, our hunger, our fears, and our desire.

I twist closed the hot water tap. I need ice-cold water. A small part of me, the one that tries so hard to convince me we are connected on a level I am struggling to comprehend, understands, but the *me*, me is frustrated and frightened beyond comprehension. What the bloody hell?

I should have said 'No' when he asked me to accompany him to his parents' home. But when I'm around him, all my walls crumble and my inhibitions take off like a spooked herd of wildebeest. I can't let us get serious for so many reasons, the main one being I am a *pissy*. I'm too afraid to give in to my desires and my heart's wish as I did that night fourteen years ago.

Thomas deserves so much more. He deserves perfect and happily ever after. That is something I am not sure I have in me to give. I've seen too much ugly. My jaded heart simply refuses to believe I can make him happy.

It'd been awkward when he left. Do we hug, or do we kiss goodbye? We gave up after several bungled attempted friendship embraces. And as always, I finished the wine, and now I'm paying for it with a throbbing head.

12

"OH THOMAS, THIS IS GORGEOUS," I CALL OVER MY shoulder from where I stand in the backyard of the three-bedroom, stone-walled A-frame house. The backyard overlooks a nature reserve filled with *fynbos*, and runs out into the bay below. King proteas are still in bloom. Their prominent pink heads dot color across the indigenous Cape shrubbery as sugar birds slurp their sweet nectar.

"It sure is. My parents built this house in Fish Hoek's early days." Thomas comes to stand beside me. "Your pa rented the house out over the years, but when the last family left six months ago, he had it re-painted and the garden cleaned up."

"That's nice of him." My eyes drink in Thomas's athletic form hugged comfortably by his blue uniform and my body begins to tingle. I look away in case he turns and sees the naughty thoughts painted across my face.

"*Ja,* he's a good man. By the way . . ."

My head snaps toward him as his tone suggests he has something to confess.

"We're going to see him after this. He has something of my father's he says is important."

"He didn't say what it is?" Ugh, Pa and his secrets.

"No. He just said and that I'll know what to do with it."

"That sounds sinister." I try to come across lighthearted.

I look back out over the *veld* and toward the distant blue, where horizon meets ocean. We're supposed to be friends, but I can feel myself being pulled deeper into Thomas's life with no way of curbing the attraction. "I hope you don't mind me asking, but why'd he wait so long before he sent you the letter about the trust and the house?"

"It wasn't him. It was my parents' wish that, if anything ever happened to them, the trust would only be given to me when I turned thirty. They wanted to make sure I was mature enough, or something like that. Honestly, I think it was their way of protecting me and the inheritance from Ibrahim," he explains, then smiles.

My legs almost give in. That dimple! "When was your birthday?"

"A few weeks ago, but I've been busy so I ignored the letter. It was only when he called me and urged me to open it that I found out about all of this." He raises both arms up beside him in a shrug.

The house is empty, but it's beautiful. I shove my hands in my denim shorts pockets as Thomas makes his way down the steps leading from the patio to the lawn, then stops and turns to face the house. His dark eyes are swirling with wonder, emotions, and other things. Things I'm not sure I want to acknowledge. He looks at me, then back at the house.

I can see he is trying to digest everything that's happened, and I know it's not only the revelation that his parents left him a piece of them in the form of photo albums, furniture, diaries, and a home. It's us too.

But I can't think on that now. This is about Thomas and him making peace with his past.

He sighs deeply, then heads inside. I follow him back indoors and to a room that is supposed to be a study of some sort. There is a simple bookshelf built into the wall in one corner, and a large bay window opposite it. Thomas says nothing, but his shoulders are tense, and by the way his eyes rove over every inch of the room, I know he's looking for something.

"Are you planning some redecorating?" I ask.

"Huh? Oh, um, no." He wanders over to the bay window and sits on the wooden ledge.

"Does it have to do with Ibrahim's interest in your folks' stuff?" I wave a hand around me.

"Yeah. I thought I was simply tying up loose ends and getting closure when I went to see him. But he kept pushing me for answers about my parents' belongings and especially the things in my father's study."

"Why? Was there anything of value in here?" My eyes scan the off-white walls and shadowed corners.

"I don't know. But I'll be dammed if I let him know all their stuff was kept safe in storage." Thomas stands, gives the room one last glance, then walks out.

Movement outside through the bay window catches my attention. It's probably a bird or one of those pesky Vervet monkeys, though I can't shake the uneasy feeling settling over me.

I push the uncomfortable sensation away and stroll through to the living area. It truly is a beautiful house. The lounge sports a fireplace and a dining room filled with light from the large windows.

I can easily imagine the warmth of a family filling it. My thoughts wander a little further and I see myself and Thomas lazing on a large couch as our children play with their blocks and books on the floor.

What the heck?

The thought shakes my very center and I go to find Thomas, who I find inspecting the staircase.

"I want to show you something." He takes my hand

in his and leads me upstairs. I follow him down the carpeted passage.

"I think . . ." He points to marks on the door. "This was me." His voice trembles.

I kneel to take in the black scribbles on the doorpost. It's clear none of the renters tried to remove it, and the layers of varnish have entombed it into the wood forever.

I read the last one.

March 22nd 1990, 2.5 years, 86 cm.

"They were killed that September." He kneels beside me. I have no words, but I squeeze his hand.

Thomas rubs a thumb up and down the handwriting with his free hand before he lets go of mine and stands. I don't make it obvious I see him wiping a tear from his cheek.

Should I hug him? I don't know what to do. Will he think I see him as weak if I do?

"Will you move in?" I hold my trembling hands behind my back as we make our way down the stairs.

He runs a hand along the narrow balustrade. I push away the yearning. I wish it was my body his hand was appreciating and not a piece of beautifully carved wood. The picture of us and our children resurfaces.

I look away, afraid my desire might show on my face.

"I don't know. I'm still getting used to the idea my parents had things and left them for me. All my life,

I've been told what a disappointment I was. Now I can see it meant nothing. I am proud to be a Campbell. My parents' journals are full of their work and passion, and *me*. I know how much I was loved and that my mother wanted nothing to do with her family, or her controlling brother."

"I'm pleased you have something left of them, Thomas. It's hard to lose a parent at any age. You say your mother wanted nothing to do with her family? What about her parents?"

"My grandfather passed before my time," he says.

We walk into the kitchen. Thomas looks around, then opens and closes the oven before strolling across to the other end and taking in the size of the pantry.

"My uncle and auntie always made sure to blame it on the fact my mother married my father."

"It must've broken your mother's heart to sever ties with her family?"

"There's a passage in one of her journals where she describes how she and my dad first met. She was quite the writer, almost lyrical. It reads more like a short romantic novel than a journal entry. Anyway, after all the romance, a dark piece follows. She tells how Ibrahim abused her verbally and threatened her with damnation and punishment. Her father, my grandfather, was a sickly man, and my grandmother was already dead. It wasn't easy for her, and according to her journal, she'd tried to keep contact with her father, but Ibrahim had seen her shunned."

I follow Thomas back into the lounge area, trying to ignore the vision I had earlier of Thomas, myself, and non-existent children. I'd never realized just how much pain and loss this man had experienced.

I look at him as he stands and takes in his surroundings. Only those with character and depth end up the way Thomas has. Strong, moral, forgiving, and kind.

"This is a home for a family." His words cause my heart to stutter.

"I'm sorry they were taken from you."

Thomas smiles. I melt . . . again!

"The path of life is different for us all, and for good reason. I don't understand why mine had to be without my parents. But I had to believe that life could be better than the one I had with the Abads and, turns out, it is. Faith is what kept me going and faith is what will keep me going through both the good times and the bad." His words echo what Pa said only a few short weeks ago.

"How is it you have faith but no religion?" My thoughts fall from my lips, and I freeze where I stand.

Thomas comes to stand in front of me. "I do not need a religion to tell me who I am or who I must be. Being a good person should come naturally and it does for most of us. When we seek and hold onto a faith, life loves us and delivers only what is good for us. That keeps our feet on the path of goodness and fulfillment.

We are what we believe. What do you believe,
Rochelle?"

I don't want to acknowledge what is so blatant. If I
do, it means all the garble the old woman mumbled is
real. All Pa's words are real. All the aching bits inside
me are real. And my feeling deserve
acknowledgement.

I know now it was never his intention to turn his
back on what we had all those years ago. But how do I
know, for certain, that we're not merely caught up in a
moment? I don't believe in visions, curses, or fate. But I
can't ignore the weirdness of us reconnecting. What if I
give in, let go, and wake up in an empty bed tomorrow?

One thing I know for sure is that I could never
survive another rejection from this man. I try to look
away, but my eyes won't listen to my brain, nor will the
rest of my body. I feel the tug on the invisible cord
between us, and I'm drawn to Thomas like the moon to
the stars. I hold my breath. I want him. I need him. But
with the dark nature of my career, all I'll ever give him
is heartbreak. How can one broken heart heal another?

Thankfully, his phone rings.

————

THOMAS NAVIGATES the car through the open gates of
Nooitgedacht. "I'm nervous."

I smile at him. "About what my pa's been keeping
safe for you?"

His hands clench the steering wheel so hard I'm waiting for it to snap like a twig. "Yeah and . . . I've not seen him since that night."

We left soon after Thomas's spiritual revelation in his home at Fish Hoek. I couldn't answer him, and didn't want to see the look of disappointment he might've had in my inability to understand what it means to have faith.

"You have nothing to worry about." I squeeze his leg, then let go as a rush of electricity surges up my arm. I don't want to add the details that my pa, the sweet old wine farmer come matchmaker, has already broached the subject of our relationship with me. It is only important that Thomas knows that Pa has no issues whatsoever about what happened that night.

"After all, aren't we just friends?" I say, more to remind myself than anything else.

Thomas doesn't look at me; he only nods. Shit, I suck at this stuff. I'm not sure how I should feel or if I can even trust my feelings. I look out the front wind-screen, and my good mood morphs into an instant thunderstorm as Thomas pulls up to the house and I spot Raymond's jalopy.

"What's the matter? It looks like you just bit into a stink bug." Thomas switches off the car and shifts in his seat to face me.

"My brother's here."

"And that's a bad thing?" He shrugs, then wipes his

forehead with a handkerchief he's pulled out of his pants pocket.

"Yes, and Pa won't discuss your matters in front of him."

I decide to enlighten Thomas about Raymond Le Roux. He'll find out anyway. Better sooner than later, before the shirt on his back has been conned out of him.

"Raymond is as slick as a newly born baby seal, only not as cute. You remember that pyramid scheme which went south a couple of years back?"

Thomas nods, and I see him put two and two together.

"Yup, all Raymond Le Roux's handiwork. He spent eight years in prison and Pa cashed in several of his policies to try and repay the people his son had scammed."

"Okay. I promise not to buy into anything he is selling."

"Also . . ."

"Yes?" The left corner of Thomas's eyebrow arches.

"My brother's not only a thieving, lying ass. He's an ignorant redneck hick." How do I explain my brother's an out-and-out racist? A man who gives all white people a bad name.

"It's all good. I've been through worse."

Has he? I place my hand on his shoulder. "Perhaps we should go."

Thomas gives me a sideways glance. "I promise, it's all good."

Pa calls out from the front door. "You're here!"

"Too late. I apologize in advance for my racist, convict brother."

Thomas laughs. "Unfortunately, none of us get to choose our family." He winks.

13

Thomas double checked his shirt was neatly tucked into his trousers and his palms were free of sweat before walking around the car to open Rochelle's door. Her astonished gaze brought a smile to his face. Chivalry had long since died, but he'd be dammed if he ever treated a woman with disrespect. He followed Rochelle up the stairs to where Derrek Le Roux stood.

"Hi, Pa." Rochelle wrapped her arms around her father before plonking a peck on his cheek.

"Hello, Spooky," *Oom* Derrek embraced his daughter.

Thomas stuck out his hand to greet the man. "Good day, *Oom* Derrek."

"Good to see you, Thomas, my boy." Derrek Le Roux grabbed his hand and pulled him into a bear-hug, as he might a long-lost son who'd returned home.

The ice, which had begun to invade his nervous

system on their way over, melted and left a warmth which spread across the scar of an old wound. It was never Rochelle or her parents, only Ibrahim who'd had an issue or felt personally affronted all those years ago.

"It's good to see you too, *Oom*. Thank you for . . ." Thomas began to broach the subject of his parents when *Oom* Derrek shook his head.

"Not now. My son will soon tire of our company."

Thomas looked to Rochelle who nodded and tried for a smile, which came out more like a grimace. Should he be that worried about her brother?

He didn't like how Rochelle paled when she'd realized her brother was here. It was more than his racist behavior she feared, he could tell. As for him, he was well versed in navigating derogatory remarks and "it was just a joke" comments. Though it had been more the Cape Malay community than white folk who had whipped him with insulting comments of his bastardness. While he had his mother's eyes and olive skin, he was lighter in coloring than most, and his hair carried with it the red sheen of his father's Scottish heritage.

The rest of the world had no understanding of the African meaning of bastard, nor the pride some gave to the word which meant half-breed just like the Rehoboth Basters of Namibia. But that was not to say it was ever spoken to him as a form of pride as a child. "You're a filthy little bastard!" was often spat at him and it had cut him deeply.

Never again.

He was proud of the people his parents were and prouder still that he'd survived all the years of adversity. As their son, he'd continue to let their good name live through him, bastard or no, and he'd no longer bare the shame but carry it as a shield.

"Come on in, you two. There's a *lekka* lamb biryani waiting with a chilled bottle of Riesling."

Derrek stopped and turned to Thomas. "Sorry, my boy, there's also Coke and fruit juice."

Thomas smiled. "Not a problem, *Oom*. I drink wine."

Oom Derrek's belly jiggled as he laughed. "Yes, of course you do." He winked and waddled off.

The inviting smell of garam masala drifted down the passage, calling to Thomas's empty belly as he followed the daughter and father to the kitchen. He'd forgotten to eat this morning. The excitement of collecting Rochelle and taking her to the house had completely doused his appetite until this moment.

He entered the kitchen to find Raymond sitting at the table as though he owned the place.

Now he understood her trepidation. Thomas recognized Raymond instantly. He was the man who'd scoped out Rochelle's apartment block last night. Why was he stalking his sister?

Thomas hid the recognition behind a blank expression and stepped forward, hand outstretched. "Good day, you must be Raymond. Pleased to meet you. I am Thomas Campbell."

Raymond barely glanced at Thomas. "What is this then?"

Rochelle came to stand beside Thomas. "I'm sorry," she whispered. "Where's your bloody manners, Raymond? You might be an ex-jailbird, but I know Pa and Ma taught you to treat others with respect," she scolded as her hands gripped her hips.

"There's no room for an attitude, Raymond." Derrek put his foot down.

"*Ja?* Well you lot enjoy the food; me? I've got better company to keep." He stood, bumping his chair over, and stomped out the house.

"*Ja,* like your *gat gabbas* from the *chooki*?" Rochelle called after him as she picked up the chair.

Raymond's backward glare suggested Rochelle had purposefully hit a nerve.

"I tried to warn you." Rochelle turned to Thomas.

People like Raymond rarely affected him. It'd been more than twenty years since apartheid was abolished, but there would always be ignorant, selfish hicks in this world, and they weren't always white either. But what he felt for her was greater than the sum of all the hatred in this world—and at the end of the day that was what truly mattered.

He met her worried gaze. "Relax. I promise I'm okay."

———

DEREK POURED the wine as Rochelle dished up. Thomas took the gap to send Janet a quick SMS. If there was one thing she was good at, it was digging up dirt on people. And he wanted the lowdown on Raymond Le Roux, like, yesterday.

The food was superb—just the right amount of spice and brown onion, and the lamb was as tender and soft as butter.

While he had no time for Trish, she'd been a damn good cook, but this meal would beat her spicy blends hands down. Though Thomas wasn't sure if it was the food, or the wonderful company which enhanced the flavors.

"So, Thomas, how is the Navy treating you, my boy?" *Oom* Derek asked, after washing down a mouth full of delicious lamb with his wine.

"Not too shabby, *Oom*. I must say, the lifestyle suits me."

"You miss sailing the seven seas now you're back on base?"

"Nah. I served my time. I get to go out every now and again for a training exercise and that's enough. Honestly, I enjoy my students more." Thomas smiled then shoved a fork full of biryani in his mouth and allowed the flavors to carry him away.

They were halfway through their meal when Raymond walked back into the kitchen, grabbed a spoon, and ate from the pot.

"I see you've forgotten what little manners you had." Rochelle poked the wounded lion.

Raymond snorted. "At least I don't take what doesn't belongs to me."

"Now, Raymond, I've told you, you've long since spoiled any chance of an inheritance," Oom Derek reminded his son.

Thomas decided to keep his attention focused on his plate of food.

"*Ja*, I see you changed the code on the safe too."

"I've sold the hunting rifles, Raymond. Besides, one of the conditions of your parole is that you not come in contact with any kind of firearm."

By the way the *Oom's* body had stiffened and his tone had chilled, Thomas guessed that might not be the reason he suspected his son was trying to open the safe.

Rochelle's back was to her brother, so only Thomas saw the warning glance she gave him. Thomas carried on eating as though he'd heard nothing, and *Oom* Derek's face remained straight as a plank.

"So, Sis, besides mixing with the lowlifes . . . you digging your new pad in that hovel behind the hospital you call home?"

Rochelle leaned back in her chair. "How'd you know where I live? You know what? Don't answer."

Thomas noticed how closely Raymond watched Rochelle's face. Her brother was after something, and it wasn't merely to make everyone uncomfortable.

"And you, Pa. You telling me you're okay with your daughter and this?" He aimed a finger at Thomas. "Is it because he's wearing a uniform you think it makes it okay?" Raymond blurted as Derrek held up a warning hand.

"So, Thomas, what wisdom is it you impart on your students?" Derrek asked, ignoring his son.

A red wave rose up Raymond's neck and washed over his face. He threw the spoon down on the table, the clatter causing everyone to stop and face him. "Ugh, your head's gone to pot, *ole toppie*! And you . . ." He pointed the same finger at Rochelle after accusing her father of being senile.

Rochelle jumped out of her chair, her right hand gripping her cotton serviette so hard her knuckles lost all color.

Raymond didn't budge. Instead, he stepped forward and stuck his face in Rochelle's. "You think you can just come back after all these years and play the favorite child again, *ne*!"

Warning tingles spread through Thomas's body as Raymond dug his finger into his sister's shoulder.

Rochelle pushed her brother away. "That's enough. Leave; get in your car and bugger off, Raymond! You and your disgusting attitude are not welcome here! And for goodness sake, take a bath!"

Thomas rose from his chair when Raymond began to laugh. Bracing himself, he could see the change in her brother's demeanor as he took on a threatening stance. *Oom* Derrek also stood, his expression unchanged.

"It's best you leave, son. You've done nothing but upset your sister and be rude to our guest."

"Guest?" Raymond stumbled back as though he'd been struck. "Guest! You *blerrie* stupid old man! That's no guest. That's a *blerrie* half-bred *hottentot*, a *gham* you allowed to sit like a white man at our table—Ma's table!"

The next few moments happened in slow-motion. Thomas watched as Rochelle pulled her arm back and brought her hand cracking across her brother's face. Raymond's head snapped to the side before a red palm print glowered on his cheek. Thomas sprinted around the table and pushed Rochelle behind him. Raymond's arm flung back, his hand balled ready to punch but got no further.

In a movement as swift as a pouncing cheetah, Thomas grabbed Raymond's fist. He twisted the arm and brought the man to his knees.

"Fffooook!" Raymond's mouth flew open and a yowl echoed through the kitchen.

"Enough!" Thomas's voice was crisp and clear enough to make certain all present knew there'd be no more nonsense.

———

ONCE THOMAS WAS SATISFIED that Rochelle was okay, he accompanied *Oom* Derrek out to the front steps. He wasn't about to let the old man have a showdown with Raymond. The pair watched Raymond speed away in a cloud of dust and a promise of revenge. Rochelle had remained in the house.

"I am so sorry. I was hoping that today of all days I could make up for what happened those many years ago."

"No, *Oom*, don't blame yourself, not for that night and not for today either. The food was *lekka,* and we have half a bottle of superb Riesling to go yet."

Oom Derrek considered Thomas, then smiled and patted a fat hand on his back. "I am pleased you and my Spooky have found one another again. I knew you would."

Thomas bit back the need to tell the *oom* he was just as happy and he hoped that things would soon progress from *only friends* to more, but thought better of it and instead, he smiled and nodded.

"Come, let's go see if Rochelle is okay." Derrek motioned for Thomas to take the lead. "That no-good son of mine won't be back anytime soon, and we have much to discuss."

Thomas's heart ached for *Oom* Derrek. The hurt his wayward son caused the old man was evident in the way *Oom* Derrek's lips paled and his eyes dimmed. What had happened that Raymond had turned out the rotten apple? Derrek and Rochelle were more than decent humans. His uncle came to mind. He guessed there was one in every family.

———————

WITH THE DISHES CLEARED, the trio sat at the kitchen table. The back door stood open, and a cool breeze drifted in from the vineyard. *Oom* Derrek emptied the last of the wine into their glasses before leaning into his chair with a glass in one hand while his other arm folded itself across his chest.

"*Och*, your dad was a great friend and an excellent cop," *Oom* Derrek explained. "He was clever and always caught his man. He was so close when . . ." The old man stumbled over a deep breath and rubbed the back of his hand across his eyes. "Agh, sorry, my boy. It hurts to remember that night." The old man's voice carried a severe sadness with it. "Do you remember much?"

Oom Derrek's question threw Thomas. Until this moment, he'd never thought of the night he'd become an orphan, not wanting to dwell too close to the dark cloud which had always resided in the back of his mind.

Thomas simply shook his head. "No, *Oom*."

"Probably best. You were so small. It was a godsend you never came to harm."

A heavy silence settled over the table as they sipped their wine and contemplated life.

"I was so sorry to see you shipped off to the man your mother spent her life trying to escape. But while your parents had left documentation for *Tannie* Anna and I to be your legal guardians, Ibrahim Abad had the judge in his pocket and got that part of your parents' wishes overruled. I only just kept his grubby paws off your inheritance."

"I've gone back to look for the police report, but the officer simply shrugged with an, '*Eish, bras, they're missing. Sorry neh.*'" A part of Thomas had been rather grateful the docket had vanished. In the past his mind had balked each time he'd tried to think back on that awful night all those years ago.

"*Ag tog.* My boy, that is part of the reason you are here today. Give me a minute. It's all locked up in my safe." He placed his glass on the table and left the kitchen.

Rochelle hadn't said a word. But if the brazen blue of her eyes and the flush in her cheeks was anything to go by, she was mad as a wounded buffalo.

He couldn't help it. He reached across the table and laid his hand on hers. "You okay?"

The lightning in her gaze softened to a calm tropical ocean. "I hate him. I know I am supposed to love him, but truly, Thomas, I hate him. I am so . . ." She began to apologize when *Oom* Derrek waddled back in, a fat, brown manila envelope in his hands.

He laid it on the table before Thomas. Black, faded ballpoint pen was scribbled across it.

Derrek. Die sleutel is in Thomas se versie. Hou dit velig todat jy dit kan gebruik.

Derrek. The key is in Thomas's nursery rhyme. Keep this safe until you can use it—the label read.

"It's addressed to you, *Oom*?" Thomas gripped the envelope.

"*Ja,* it is. But I've never taken it to the authorities—not while Ibrahim was your guardian, and not until I was certain you were in a position where he could no longer harm you." Derrek sat back down and reached for his wine, gulped half of it and leaned back into his chair. "Probably best if you open it here so I can answer any questions you will have," he said.

Thomas stared at the words on the envelope as his right index finger stroked the letters. His father had penned this. His father's hands had touched this envelope once. A coldness spread through Thomas as the reality of what he'd lost began to resurface.

"Are you okay, Thomas?" Rochelle came to sit beside him.

Thomas nodded. "My rhyme?" he muttered.

"I remember your mother used to sing you a lullaby. She called it Thomas's Rhyme," *Oom* Derrek said. "Can you remember?"

"No, can you?"

"Sorry, my boy, I can't. It was so long ago."

14

"You're quiet." I can't stand the silence which has come to sit between us like a smelly vulture.

"This is all so much to take in. The information in that envelope." Thomas points to the manila folder on my lap without looking away from the road.

"I can only try to understand. And you so didn't need my asshole brother's vitriol either."

"Stop apologizing, Rochelle. You know if I had taken you to my uncle and auntie's house, it would have been the same. Well, no fist fighting, but they're as narrow-minded as Raymond. I told you how they shunned my mother and father."

He has a point, but sitting beside my concern for Thomas is an anger so ripe and ready to explode all over Raymond, it takes all my willpower to douse it.

Thomas pulls into a parking bay outside my apartment building. It's almost midnight and the sun has just set. The streetlights throw an ominous orange glow onto the quiet sidewalk.

"Want to come up? I bought some decent brew the other day."

Thomas frowns.

"Coffee, sorry. Pa always calls the good stuff brew." I smile.

"Sounds great." He smiles back ,then gently takes my hand in his. "I know all that's happened between us is . . ."

"A lot to take in?" I squeeze his hand with mine. "Thomas, we're not important right now. This is." I pat the envelope still sitting patiently on my lap.

"Of course what's happening between us is important, Rochelle. How could it not be?" he asks incredulously.

His eyes are dark with soft gold spots circling his irises. They pin me to my seat. The skin on my arms breaks out in goosebumps. My breath hitches in the back of my throat. Life outside the car slows and sensations, like a myriad of blossoming buds in the *fynbos*, erupt between us.

He tugs on my hand and I fall toward him. Our lips meet. Blossoms bloom into sparks, which erupt into flames. Seconds feel like eons as our tongues collide in a frenzied need. He gives, I take, and then I give back. My hands travel over his defined torso; his cup my breast. Passion as I've never known it bursts into life and threatens to devour me entirely.

A speeding car breaks the moment and reminds us both we're smooching in the car out on the street.

I pull away. "Perhaps some coffee?"

I can't deny the feelings I've carried inside my fractured heart all these years any longer. The yearning, the need. But I can't give myself over to him like a lovestruck teenager either. Especially not when Thomas has so much baggage of his own to deal with at present.

He shifts in his seat, then looks over his shoulder through the driver's window. Something about the way he scans our surroundings sends a shiver up my legs and into my spine. "Let's go up."

I nod, and we get out of the car. I swipe the toggle over the green blinking eye of the small grey box attached to the security gate, and it clicks open.

Inside the lift, Thomas turns to face me. "That night." He places both hands on my shoulders.

"My sixteenth birthday?"

"*Ja.*" He smiles and tucks the wayward blue-colored strand of hair behind my ear. His fingers don't pull away. Instead, they trace my jawline to my lips. Goodness, if I weren't so damn afraid of all that could go wrong, I'd have him take me here and now in the lift.

"You're the most beautiful soul I've ever known."

"So are you Thomas, and brave." The last word hitches in my throat as the memory of what he's shared with me returns.

Thomas shakes his head, "No my darling. There

are few who give the way you do. So unconditional, passionately, fully."

Thomas places a tender kiss on my lips, then pulls away just enough so he can say, "That night is what reminded me to keep all that was good in life close to my heart and to never let it go."

"I thought we'd already remembered the good and the bad of it?"

Thomas leans closer so the skin of his lips are a millimeter away from mine and the tips of our noses touch, "I'm remembering the way you stood off in the corner. So . . ."

"Angry? I was so pissed Pa had arranged that stupid meeting on my birthday. My sweet sixteenth, of all things."

"I remember wondering why a beautiful girl was alone and upset. In that moment, my life changed. In that moment, I took the first step in the direction destiny had mapped out for me. For us."

The elevator pings and the doors slide open. We walk in silence to my apartment door. I'm not sure I'm ready for this conversation. My mind is battling to digest all that's happened today. I slip the key into the lock and open the security gate, followed by the front door. I flip a switch and the lounge, kitchen, and teeny-weeny dining room light up. "Brew?"

"Sounds great."

I busy myself with the coffee. I don't think I can cope with what he is about to say. I haven't been able to face the truth for so long and I have no idea how to do it now.

I look away as I say, "You turned my world as I knew it on its head, and as hard as I tried to, I could never turn it back."

Thomas comes to stand so close to me I can almost feel his heart beating in his chest. "And you mine. But perhaps we weren't meant for a right-side-up kinda life?"

I want to believe him, to hear the truth in his words. For him . . . us to be what I've yearned for all these years. But my fear gets the better of me. All common sense flees, and I am left with only my shattered sixteen-year-old self. "I can't lose myself to you again, Thomas! I won't be able to claw my way back to the light a second time."

His brown eyes light up like a bonfire, and his neck flushes in a color I can only liken to the simmering coals in a fire. "I never meant to break your heart in the first place. I've tried to love others, but there is no room for anyone else inside of me except for you."

His words slice through my center.

He steps away and wipes his hands over his face. "I know you feel what I do. Surely there is nothing to fear if we . . . I know you feel the same."

I don't hear his logic, nor do I hear his pain and bravery. I only hear my fear. I only feel the gut-wrenching hurt of a frightened teen. "You deserve more than who I am. You're a survivor; a warrior. Me, I'm a chickenshit!"

Thomas pauses, sighs, then steps toward me. "You are my brave one. I've been a walking block of ice these last fourteen years . . . until the day I saw you."

Fear and an ailing ego are ugly creatures. Together they stand sentinel to the gates of my heart.

"I think you should go." I can't look at him, but I can feel the heat of his gaze on my face.

"We're not done, Rochelle. You hold my heart in the palm of your hand and I know I hold yours too. I swear to you on my life, I'll never drop it again."

I can only watch as he respects my stupid, irrational wish, turns around, and leaves me. This time it's because I asked him to.

———

THOMAS DROVE as though an armada were after him. He did not care if the cops stopped him. He did not care if his car hit a pothole and he was knocked into oblivion.

Why, why had he left? He knew why . . . that look in her eyes, the one which reminded him of a sad, wounded animal. It was all him. He was kidding himself thinking he could win her back. Sometimes there were hearts that could never be mended, and he had broken hers.

Thomas slowed his sedan as he drove up to the gate of the barracks. It was a dark night. The full moon hid her mournful gaze behind a thick blanket of fog and sullen stars. It reminded Thomas of all those lonely months after meeting Rochelle. How dark and desolate his life had felt without her, without being able to even tell her why. *Och*, was love worth all this nonsense?

"Good evening, Lieutenant. In a hurry?"

Thomas pulled out his naval identification as he stopped at the security gate of the base. "No, Seaman, just a *blerrie* woman."

The young man, from Xhosa decent, was one of Thomas's best students. An orphan and a go-getter like himself.

"*Eish*, in that case, sir, you should join Mosedi in the officer's bar."

Thomas frowned. "How so, Seaman Ntebe?"

"The poor man caught his lady with another . . ." He leaned toward Thomas and with his hand cupped around his mouth whispered, "Lady."

Thomas bit back a laugh. The man had an almost theatrical manner of conveying information, especially when it came to gossip. Same-sex relationships were not as easily accepted in African cultures as the world would like to believe.

"I think I'll be safer on my own. Thank you."

The seaman straightened and saluted. "Sir, yes, sir. I reckon his head's gonna be *yayinzima kakhulu* in the morning." The seaman rubbed his head to indicate the slighted officer's impending hangover.

Both men laughed . Thomas pulled away and drove to his barracks. At this point, he might just choose a sore head over a sore heart.

He parked his car and grabbed the envelope *Oom* Derrek had given him, then made his way to the dorms. Unlike men of lower rank, he had his own room.

Thomas closed and locked the door behind him. He stripped off his casual uniform and pulled on a pair of rugby shorts and a T-shirt.

He sat on his bed and allowed the day's happenings to flow through him. The bright afternoon at his parents' home, the dinner at *Nooitgedacht*, and the revelations of the information *Oom* Derrek had handed him. He pushed aside the ache in the center of his being. Did it really have to end the way it had?

He would go so far as to admit he loved her, but could what he felt be enough for them both?

One thing he was sure of was that he needed to go through the evidence his father had gathered with his mother's help. Evidence which implicated a man whose description came very close to that of his uncle, Ibrahim Abad. It all centered on a syndicate based in Simon's Town specializing in arts and human trafficking, the likes of which the world had never seen before. What was more worrisome was that Thomas was convinced the syndicate his father had been investigating all those years ago was one in the same as the trafficking ring currently causing them grief.

Was this the reason Ibrahim had tried to "reconnect"—to find out what Thomas knew? The evidence pointing to Ibrahim was circumstantial at best, but his father had been onto something. And then there was the cryptic message scrawled across the envelope. Thomas's rhyme? Would his mother have written it down in one of her diaries? If Ibrahim truly sat behind all this duplicity, Thomas would have to tread carefully.

Thomas stood, walked over to his cupboard, before unlocking it. He knelt and moved the rucksack out of the way to reveal a small safe. As his fingers danced across the keypad, he tried to remember the rhyme mentioned in the message to *Oom* Derrek. The lock clicked, and he tugged open the heavy door. Inside the small safe lay a stack of books: his mother and father's diaries.

After an hour of turning pages, Thomas came up with less than nothing. His eyes burned, and his neck ached.

Lying back on his bed, his eyelids dropped shut and he allowed the essence of his parents to seep into his mind. Sucking in a deep breath, he commanded his muscles to relax and his memories to travel back . . .

Thomas drifted into the black hole, letting it swallow him.

A voice, soft and sweet, echoed off the dark walls of his memories . . .

Monday's child . . .

His mother's voice whispered as the past flitted back, one word at a time. The old children's verse drifted to the surface on his mother's lyrical voice.

A face as bright as the moon and as beautiful as the stars around it floated above him...

The rain pounded a warning as it pelted down on the roof of his childhood home. "It's okay *Nunu*. Shh, shh, now." His mother pulled him from his warm bed and shoved him into the back seat of the car. "We'll be safe once we get there." His father's voice, comforted. The car took off at speed, pushing small Thomas into his seat, then skidded to a stop. His mother screamed... gunshots... large hands reach into the car and rip his parents away . . .

A voice. One which his three-year-old mind had not known then, but his adult self knew now!

Thomas sat bolt upright.

His breath fled his chest as realization knocked him back. Was Ibrahim Abad behind his parents' deaths?

God, he'd been there. He'd heard the shots which had robbed him of his parents' love. But he could not remember the faces of the men, and their voices were nothing more than mumbles . . . except for that one.

Oom Derrek hadn't said it in so many words. Now he thought back to all the conversations he'd had with the old man. The subtle hints he'd dropped. Everything was smoke and mirrors. But Thomas was determined to prove his uncle sat behind his parents' deaths.

Heart racing and with his T-shirt drenched in sweat, Thomas decided on a run. He needed to clear his head and plan his next move.

15

MY EYES POP OPEN AT THE SHRILL CALL OF MY PHONE. I reach out toward my bedside table and feel around until my fingers find the slim surface of the device. My mind is foggy after a terrible night's sleep.

"He-hello . . ."

"Rochelle, it's Rudy . . . Dr. Ekstein. Listen, girl, they've just rushed your dad in. We suspect a farm attack. By the looks of it he's sustained a massive blow to the side of his head. You had better hurry."

My body snaps to attention and I sit bolt upright. "On my way!"

God, please, I know I've pushed you away, but don't let him die! Don't take him away from me.

I pray as I pull open drawers, rip random pieces of clothing from them, and begin to dress. There's no time to comb the knots out, so I pile my hair on top of my head and shove an elastic around it.

My world's been upended, and this time it is not of my doing. I find my keys sprawled out on the kitchen counter. I haven't got time to remove the sticky substance that's clung to them these last few days.

I rush from my apartment. It'll take me less time on foot than first running down to the garage and driving.

I'm out of the elevator the moment the doors begin to open and practically bowl one of the residents over.

"Soreee!" I call out, but do not stop until I reach the outer security gate.

The silly toggle won't work. I rub it between my hands and try again. Nothing.

"*Fok tog!*" I shout at the irritating contraption and rattle it.

I calm and take a deep breath, then slide the toggle down again. This time the lock releases, and I fling it open with so much force it bangs against the iron security fence and everything vibrates.

I take off down the street at a sprint. At the corner, I make a sharp right and nail it all the way until I reach the traffic light at the end of the block. It's just after five a.m. The sun's sitting level on the eastern horizon. Her red and gold beams echo the warning lights of an ambulance. My heart's still aching from the silly argument I had with Thomas last night. But that has to wait.

I make it to the hospital in record time and reach for my phone to send Thomas a text, then remember how I ended things and return it to my jeans pocket. I sprint through the large, open sliding doors of the emergency department.

"Doctor Le Roux." A young nurse runs up to me.

"Where is he, Pauline?" I push past.

"He's been rushed up for a CT Scan."

I skid to a stop. "What happened?" I grab the poor nurse by the shoulders.

Pauline lifts her hands and gently removes mine. "All we can make out from his housekeeper"—she nods over to Grace, who is as pale as porridge, standing nearby—"is that she was the one who found the front door open and your father lying in a pool of blood in the study. They suspect a traumatic brain injury. He'd been hit with what we think is the butt of a hand gun on the occipital region of his skull."

I don't have to give it a second thought. "Raymond!"

"Excuse me, Doctor?"

"Has my brother been here?"

"I didn't know you had a brother, Doctor."

The next half an hour plays out in automated motion.

The police arrives and two officers question both me and Grace.

"We'll need the last known address for your brother, but it would seem there was more than one attacker present," the constable doesn't look up from her notepad as she speaks.

"More than one?"

The cop gives me a sideways glance. "You have no

idea where your brother lives?" The constable repeats her question.

"Why do you think there was more than one attacker?"

"From the evidence collected."

I have to bite my tongue as the words, *well duh, Sherlock,* itch to bounce off my lips, with the urge to slap the constable.

I need to get to Pa. I seriously don't have time for this crap! "No, officer. I do not know where Raymond Le Roux lives. I saw him for the first time in ten years at my father's residence a few days ago and again at an early dinner yesterday. Before that, he was a guest of the state in jail. We aren't exactly close." I roll my eyes. "Can I go now?"

"No, you can go as soon as I have everything I need." The bloody stubborn-as-hell constable places her hand on my arm, and I give her a warning glance.

"I'll call up to Radiology and check for you." Pauline hushes my boiling temper.

"Thanks." I wrap my arms around myself as the corner of my eye catches Grace, now sitting on a chair in the corner, shaking.

"We can take a seat while you ask all your questions." I tell the young policewoman.

She nods, and I make my way to where Grace is. I sit beside her and place my hands in hers.

"*Eish*, Shelly. Derrek was almost another number on those white crosses." She refers to a nearby hill where white crosses stand vigil, dedicated to every single farm murder victim of the last twenty-four years. The image is like a knife to my heart.

Grace lays her head on my shoulder and weeps.

"It's okay, Gracie." I try to console her. "He's going to be okay," I say more to convince myself than the weeping, bewildered Grace. Was this another farm attack? Or did Raymond have something to do with it?

"Now, Dr. Le Roux, do you know of any disgruntled workers?" The constable continues with her line of questioning.

It irritates me that the copper can't look up from her notebook. *Make eye contact, you sod!*

"*Haaiman! Sonke sivuyiswe kwi-nooitgedacht! Uya kwenza ngcono khangela abo baphanga baze babulale abalimi.*" Grace goes off at the constable in her mother's tongue of Xhosa. She tells the woman in no uncertain terms that she is sniffing in the wrong place.

"I'll need a list of employees," the constable requests, ignoring Grace's tirade.

"Sure, but first I need to make a call." I pull my phone from my pocket.

Stuff my pride!

The ED doors slide open twenty minutes later and Thomas rushes in, ignoring the unit manager, the cop, and the security officer who try to stop him as he makes a bee line for me.

His arms are like a cloak of steel as they wrap around my body.

"Are you okay?" He leans back and inspects me with eyes full of concern.

I can't speak, afraid I might burst in to tears, so I nod.

"Where's your pa?"

I simply point up with my finger. I wait for him to tell me how silly I was last night and brace myself. Instead he pulls me back in to his arms as the constable attempts to continue her questioning.

The warmth of his body dissolves my resolve, and tears run down my cheeks. I cry, not sure for how long, but he cradles me like a fragile, precious piece of porcelain. And for a few moments, I allow myself to let go of the hurt, the loss, and my worry. Sometimes a woman's allowed to feel vulnerable.

For the first time in years, I feel safe. It's an earth-shattering sensation.

———

It's after midday when Pa is wheeled out of theatre and into the intensive care unit. He is in an induced coma. Tubes run from his arms and from beneath the sheet to bags hanging beside him and above his head. He is on life support. A large ribbed tube snakes its way from his lips to a machine breathing for him. I have treated many severe and life-threatening cases in my life, but seeing Pa lying there crushes my very being.

"Wait out here till we get him comfortable," the ICU nurse instructs.

I know how important it is to stay out of their way. But it's hard to remain composed when all I want to do is run in after her and make sure they do things right. They will, they're great at what they do, but . . .

I turn to look over my shoulder. Thomas is making his way toward me, dressed in blue camos with two coffees in hand.

"Grace is home." He places the warm double dirty chai latte in my hands. He'd offered to take her home once the police were satisfied all their questions were answered.

"Thank you." I lean into him. "I'm sorry about last night," I whisper into his chest.

"Me too."

"Was it a problem for you to leave work?" I ask, then sip my drink.

"No, we'd just finished a planning exercise, and I told them it was a family emergency."

"Oh." I nod, wondering what a planning exercise was.

Thomas, ever the vigilant, reads my expression. "I can't give you specifics, but basically it's when a bunch of us who are specialists in our field are asked to come up with a solution to a problem."

"Oh," I mutter as the door opens and the nurse, a woman I suspect is in her early forties, dressed in clean light blue scrubs, waves me in. "Come in when you're ready. Don't forget to sanitize your hands."

I take another sip of my coffee and turn to Thomas.

"I'll wait out here . . . unless you need me." Thomas pulls me against him one last time. I am torn between wanting to be by my Pa and needing Thomas's warm protectiveness wrapped around me a little longer.

I stand on my toes and place a thank you kiss on his lips, then hand him my cup, and walk to the door.

The ICU is one of the largest in the Cape Province. Its stark white walls and beeping instruments bring home the reality of how dangerously close I am to losing my father. The cutting smell of antiseptic and starched linen, with a side order of sickly bodies, drifts up my nose. My legs wobble and I have to lean against the nurse's station.

"Are you okay?" the nurse asks with a hand on my shoulder.

I nod. "*Ja.* It's just been a rough morning."

"I understand. If he makes it through tonight, he'll be fine."

I know this, but it helps to hear it confirmed, though her unconvincing smile twists my gut.

I let go of the counter and stumble toward the bed in the corner.

For the first time in all my years in medicine, my stomach roils and flips.

Pa is as white as the sheet covering him.

I pick up his file and read the notes. I swallow the nauseated nerves punching their way up my throat.

And then I sigh with relief. Although Pa received an almighty knock to the back of his head, causing some bleeding and swelling on the occipital lobe, it had been minimal. The second bash to the side of his head was similar. His ear had taken the brunt of the trauma. He'd suffered a perforated eardrum. Thankfully, Pa had not stopped breathing or lost too much blood to deprive him of any oxygen.

I try to see the glass half full.

With great surgery, which he's received, and good nursing, Pa should make a full recovery. I can't help but feel sorry for the rehabilitation therapist though. I smile as I think of how stubborn my dear father can be.

After helping the nurse bathe and treat any potential pressure areas on Pa's body, I say my goodbyes. I lean down and whisper my promise to pop in later that evening. Pa's forehead is a little cool to the touch when I kiss him good night, and he smells of antibiotics, antiseptics and anesthesia.

"Perhaps I should stay," I utter, more to myself than anyone else.

"Go home and get some rest; there is nothing more you can do. I promise he is in safe hands," the nurse assures me as she leads me to the doors.

I'm not comfortable being the family of a patient. It's so much easier having all the answers as a doctor.

"Keep the faith, Doctor. Come morning, all will be bright and sunny once more." The nurse gives me a hug and waves me off.

Armed only with the feeling that I must believe all will be well, I exit the unit and fall into Thomas's open arms.

16

THOMAS DROVE ROCHELLE OUT TO HER PA'S FARM. HIS thoughts raced through his mind at a hundred miles per hour.

Janet had come back to him with information about Raymond. Though much of it was general knowledge, it bugged him that Janet had found out Raymond owed a local gang money for drugs.

He'd just have to be on the look out for that piece of scrap. Chances were he could be the culprit of his father's attack.

He'd also handed over the documents and evidence his father had collected concerning the art- and the human-trafficking ring to his superior officer. While the evidence in itself was close to thirty years old, when they'd verified it, it was proven to be as relevant now as it was then.

"This information is invaluable, Thomas. Have you

figured out the rhyme and its relevance as yet?" the rear admiral had asked.

"No, unfortunately not."

"And this man, this Ibrahim Abad, he is involved in the local council, is he not?" Captain Mosele of the SAS Protea had asked.

"Yes, and he is . . . *was* my mother's brother and the man who raised me after their deaths."

His statement had caused some ruckus and consternation.

"We can only hope his involvement will not endanger you, or our exercise. And while we've been loath to invite them, we've had to involve local law enforcement. I'm just hoping the men and women we chose and verified are not traitors," the Captain had added. This statement, though relevant, had twisted in Thomas's gut.

"Perhaps it is best if I remove myself from further planning? I believe you have all that is needed currently?" Thomas had decided to step away, before it was decided for him. That way he showed he was playing open cards and had removed himself from any connections with Ibrahim.

"Your leadership in your decision and also your actions are duly noted, Lieutenant," the rear admiral had added before Rochelle's call had come through.

Now that he had removed himself from further planning exercises and taken two days leave, he had time to spend with Rochelle. That was good, except for the fact that he could not lay to rest his suspicions of who sat behind *Oom* Derrek's attack.

————

"I NEED to check if anything was taken. That constable said I should let her know as soon as I can." Rochelle's voice was a mere whisper.

He pulled to a stop in the drive. Yellow tape spanned the width of the doorway. Rochelle got out, leaned forward, and retched. Thomas ran around to come stand beside her. "I can do it if you want?" His gesture was from his heart more than his head. He'd have no idea what possessions were missing.

"No, just don't leave me." Fear and sadness circled like hungry sharks in the depths of her sea-green gaze.

Thomas wrapped his arms around her. "It'll be okay. I'm here. I'll not leave you," he whispered into her ear.

Rochelle ripped the yellow tape from the door and unlocked it. They stepped inside.

The house was a mess. The attackers had left no stone unturned. A subtle aroma of copper and sickly sweet fermented sugar greeted them as they waded through the disarray left by the intruders.

"Where does your Pa keep the safe?" Thomas asked.

"This way, in the study." Rochelle took his hand in hers.

"Dear God!" Rochelle gasped and fell to her knees. A black pool of what could only have been *Oom* Derrek's blood soaked the light brown carpet. The tangy smell of copper increased tenfold, and a handful of blowflies circled like vultures.

Thomas kneeled down beside Rochelle. "Go wait in the car."

"I can do this." She reached out and gripped his shoulder.

"Do you really think your brother's capable? I mean, I know he has a history, but this?" Thomas motioned to the house. "It's his own father."

"I don't know, and the cops said they suspected more than one attacker. I don't want to think he is."

Thomas walked over to the safe. It was obvious whoever came to rob *Oom* Derrek had succeeded in getting him to open his safe. The grey iron door was still open, and all the contents spread out across the study.

———

THOMAS FOLLOWED Rochelle out to the car and opened the door. He watched as she wiped her eyes and nose with a tissue. He had to tell her.

"Look. I had a friend look into Raymond." He waited for Rochelle to digest his confession.

"What did this friend find?" Her voice was a mere whisper.

"No more than you already know, except that he owes a local gang money for drugs."

"That bloody arsehole! I knew he was using again!" Rochelle stomped her foot then slammed a hand against the bodywork of her four-by-four.

She was so brave, and so beautiful. He couldn't help but reach out and pull her into a warm embrace. "Come. let's get you back to your pa. And then into bed. Uh . . ."

Rochelle chuckled into his chest. It was like the ringing of a thousand fairy bells.

"I didn't mean . . ."

She leaned back, offering him one of her bright, sparkling grins. "I know what you meant, silly. But I would appreciate it if you stayed over. Are you working tomorrow?"

"No, I've taken the next two days off to be with you."

"You shouldn't waste your holidays on me."

"Rochelle Le Roux, it is no waste. I'd do it again in a heartbeat. Besides, I have other business to take care of."

Rochelle squinted her eyes the way she always did when she was thinking. "You're not going to play the hero and do something impulsive, are you?"

"Who me? *Nooit*, never! I'm as innocent as a newborn baby." He tried for humor, but knew that Rochelle saw right through him.

Yes, he'd initially taken the days off to be with her

and her pa, but he'd also decided to use the time to dig deeper into his parents' murders. His gut told him Ibrahim sat behind all this violence. It was an instinct he'd long since learned to trust.

———

THE DRIVE back to the hospital was quiet. Thomas was pleased when Rochelle dozed off for the half an hour it took to return. There were dark rings under her eyes, which worried him. It was a terrible feeling to know there was only so much he could do.

He pulled into the hospital's parking area and stopped the car. "We're here." He stroked her face gently.

Rochelle's eyelids fluttered as she yawned and sat up straight.

"Go up and see your pa. I'll get us something to eat."

"Thanks." She leaned forward and placed her warm glossy lips on his.

Once he was sure Rochelle was safely inside, Thomas drove to the local hamburger joint down the street. His mind tumbled over everything that had transpired since her phone call that morning.

Before he'd left, he'd made sure all his parents' documents, diaries, and other important papers were locked in the safe at the bottom of his cupboard. Ibrahim's reach stretched far, but he was certain the man was unable to touch the Navy. He'd also double checked his cupboard room door was locked. His precautions were more about the evidence Thomas had handed over to his superiors than *Oom* Derrek being another farm attack statistic.

He stepped inside the takeaway shop and ordered two large cheeseburgers, chips, double-thick bubblegum milkshakes, and a tub of caramel crunch ice crème. She would need her frozen escape after a day like today.

Thomas paid and went to sit on a plastic chair in the corner. The place smelled like old oil, and the floors were grey and greasy, but they made a helluva burger, and their chips were out of this world. He'd never gotten food poisoning from ordering here. He reckoned all the deep frying killed anything that might try to kill him.

Thomas's phone vibrated. "Good afternoon, Rear Admiral."

"Good afternoon, Lieutenant Campbell. It is my understanding that you have taken two days leave?"

"Yes, sir." Thomas couldn't help but wonder what issue there could be with him taking some downtime, and why Penlevan would call and not his CO from the base. Unless . . .

"I will need to revoke that."

"Is there a problem, sir?"

"Not per se, and not with you, Lieutenant Campbell. This is not a discussion for the phone. I will need you to come in tomorrow morning."

"Yes, sir."

"O' seven hundred hours, Lieutenant. At the planning bunker."

"Yes, sir."

"And Lieutenant? Watch your six."

The line went dead, and Thomas sat staring at his phone as if the damn thing had just bitten off his ear.

What the hell? He was being called in to duty and told by the admiral he should watch his back. Had the information he'd given them led to a breakthrough?

Good thing Rochelle had asked him to stay over tonight. But how would he protect her tomorrow?

Thomas opened the necessary application then typed in a message, and pressed send.

His order number was called out before he could ponder the issue any further. Thomas grabbed the bag and walked back to his car, before driving to the hospital. He sent Rochelle a message letting her know he'd wait in the reception downstairs.

He didn't enjoy the smell of hospitals. It made him uneasy and brought back faint memories of him as a small boy, sitting on a chair in a large area much like the emergency department, the night his parents had been killed.

After the night before, when he'd crossed the line his subconscious had drawn, memories from so long ago now seemed to trickle to the forefront of his mind at the most inopportune times.

Though the recollection was foggy and dim, being back in the hospital under such emotional circum-stances triggered images he'd never had. They were uncomfortable memories. Some things, Thomas real-ized, were buried in the depths of his three-year-old mind with good reason.

17

"OH, THAT WAS GREAT." I RUB MY TUMMY AND LEAN BACK into my lumpy couch. "Me and my food baby thank you." I smile at Thomas, who's shoving the last bite of his cheeseburger into his mouth.

I look a little closer. Something's bothering him. I saw it as I made my way toward him in the hospital foyer.

"*Ja*, absolutely! Damn good nosh that," he mumbles, smiles half-heartedly, and rubs his belly before wiping his mouth with a paper napkin. He downs a large slurp of his shake. "Best takeaway in Simon's Town. The boys always go there after a big night out. The oil chills their *babalas* a bit."

The same cure I know to be true for a hangover. "It's a well-known myth, and one which actually works, that an oily breakfast the morning after the night before stitches you up just fine for the day ahead. Like

Pa's *babalas* shake." I remember the sour grape and paracetamol concoction Pa made me the other morning and shudder.

We both laugh, but his isn't as full-bellied as it has always been—something is definitely wrong.

"You don't have to stay if you don't want to, Thomas." I finally gather my courage and say what I think must be bothering him.

"Why would you say that? I want to be here." He frowns and places his empty milkshake container back on the coffee table.

"Because something is worrying you. You're not . . . you."

"That obvious, huh?"

"Like a *blerrie* neon sign, bro." I sit up and ready myself for the inevitable. I knew it was all too good to be true.

"My rear admiral called this afternoon and revoked my leave. I need to clock in at seven tomorrow morning."

The apprehension which had filled my heart evaporates and leaves me somewhat deflated. "Oh." Here we go with my single-syllable replies once again.

"The thing is, I was warned."

"About what? Are you in trouble?" Now he has my full attention.

"Not with the Navy. But I was told to watch my back."

"Does it have to do with the information you gave them?"

"Well, that's the logical answer. Rochelle, I need you to do me a favor tomorrow please?"

"Anything."

"Stay at the hospital. I've arranged with a friend of mine to place a police guard outside the ICU."

The seriousness of his tone causes my stomach to lurch. "Surely that's not necessary. The hospital has great private security and ..."

"Until I know what's unfolding, I'm not taking any chances."

"I would've thought someone like Ibrahim would have the cops in his back pocket." I am so not comfortable with being told what to do, but I get that Thomas is worried about my safety.

"Not this one; that I can assure you," Thomas says as he stands.

I don't like this side of him—the stern commander. "I'm not one of your lackeys on the ship who simply follows orders." The words slip from my mouth before I can stop them, but I'm scared and frustrated.

Thomas looks down. The deep chocolate of his gaze stirs, and the golden flecks shine brighter, as the skin between his eyes creases. He comes to sit by my side. "No, you're not, and that is not what I meant."

I watch as he grapples internally with his reply.

His hands slip forward and grip mine. "You're the

woman I love, and I'll be dammed if I allow anyone to harm you or your pa. Is that understood?"

His words sink in. *The woman he loves.* I can't breathe. Instead, I pull my hands from his, pick up the cardboard cup, and down the last frothy, creamy suds of my bubble gum milkshake. Better to slurp milkshake than to gawk at him like a zombie.

Thomas holds his breath. He needs more than me slurping and ignoring his confession.

I put the empty cup back and face him. No more running. It's now or never, Rochelle Chickenshit Le Roux.

"Me too." My voice is barely audible, but I've never spoken truer words in my life.

Silence descends as the weight of what we've revealed to one another sinks in.

"How'd you guess?"

"Guess what?" Thomas smiles. His assuredness has been replaced by the nerves of the teenage boy who kissed me all those years ago.

God, this man is beautiful.

I can't help myself and shift closer to him. "That a bubblegum, not a strawberry or chocolate, but a bubblegum shake would do the trick?"

As suddenly as the boy in him appeared, so does it vanish and is replaced by a man.

In one swift move, he pulls me onto him. My legs instinctively straddle his waist and I come face-to-face with the soul I have fallen in love with for the second time in my life.

"The same way I know you'll love that tub of caramel crunch in the freezer later tonight."

"Oh, dear Lord. I'm a goner!"

Our laughter tapers off as our eyes search each other's. I allow my fingers to trace the fine lines stretching into his temples and the curve of his bottom lip. How could I not have seen it there from the first? When a man loves you truly, madly, unconditionally, it sits like an untouched diamond in the center of his soul.

"I loved you from the moment I saw you. I didn't need some old wives' tale to make it so. It was you. Always you, Rochelle." Thomas's words wash over me like the cool waters of a mountain spring. They rinse away years of anger, doubt, and rejection. "Only now do I realize all that time apart, I was living half a life. It was like trying to breathe under water, like fighting my way through a thick mountain mist."

"I've never felt so connected to any human in my life," I say as I lean down, one hand slipping from his face and around his neck, the other grasping his T-shirt.

His lips are hot and sweet, his mouth delicious and inviting. I press on him and into him. I will our clothes to disintegrate. I need to feel his smooth caramel skin on mine.

With a gentle, dexterous strength, he places his

hands under my bum and stands. My legs wrap themselves around his body. I don't end our kiss. I dare not,
for fear it might end what I so desperately need to,
want to happen between us with every inch of my soul.

———

THOMAS WASN'T sure he was heading in the right direction as he stumbled, eyes shut, kissing the woman of
his dreams. Yes, quite literally, his dreams.

"Left, straight . . ." Rochelle mumbled into his
mouth.

It became easier once he was in the short passage
connecting her bedroom, the bathroom, and the front
rooms.

"*Eina*!" he called into her mouth as his shins
connected with the bed. Her head whipped back, and
her chest heaved with laughter.

"Sorry. I laugh when I'm nervous."

"Nervous?"

She slid off him and knelt on the bed, her head
cocked as she peered at him from beneath long black
lashes. The tip of her pink tongue ran along her strawberry lips, and her nipples pressed into his chest. His
hand slid up her neck and knotted into her candy-
colored hair. He pressed his mouth down on hers and
drank from the sweet ambrosia she offered.

He leaned back, breathless, and stroked a finger
down the sharp edge of her jaw, across her lips, soft as

velvet and swollen from their kiss. Her eyes shone cat-like in the dark.

Everything he'd known to do with women in the past fled his memory. Rochelle pinched the hem of his T-shirt between her thumbs and index fingers and lifted it over his head. Her lips came onto his chest, laying delicate pecks across each collarbone and down, down. He grabbed her before she reached his belt buckle and pulled her back upright.

He undid her blouse, one agonizing button at a time. She groaned, and he reveled in her need. This goddess, this lily of the valley, wanted *him*, desired *him*, loved *him*. That was all he needed in life. The knowledge that right in this moment they were together, lingering in a haze of beauty and passion—a moment he'd waited so very long for.

18

The roar of the ocean pulled Thomas from a deep, satiated slumber. It was a clear night and the moon smiled down on the lovers from her twinkling corner of the heavens in all her hunter's glory.

Rochelle had pulled open the curtains and the window before they'd finally settled in to sleep. Thomas lifted his head as Rochelle, her blond, fairy-tinted hair spread like a blanket across them both, huddled closer. Was this a dream? Had fortune at last decided to smile on him?

Within a week, his entire life had done a one-eighty. From a lonely naval officer who had no heritage and belonged nowhere, to a man who finally had answers about who he was and where he came from. Not to mention the fact he now shared a bed with his soul mate.

They had spent hours exploring and enjoying one

another. Rochelle, with her passionate hunger, had fulfilled every fantasy he'd ever had. Thoughts of their rambunctious play stirred the muscle between his legs. He didn't want to wake her, but he was not about to pounce on her like a predator either. Perhaps some feathered kisses along her neck would rouse her enough for him to ask if she was willing? He also hoped he had at least one more condom in his pant pocket.

A sound from the lounge drew his attention.

Careful not to wake Rochelle, Thomas slipped out of bed, felt around in the gloom for his boxers, and pulled them on. The carpeted floor smothered his footsteps as he made his way toward the front room of the tiny apartment. Thomas could just make out the shape of a man, his fair hair glinting in the silver light.

Raymond!

Before the intruder knew what hit him, Thomas dove and tackled the bloke. They landed on top of the small coffee table which instantly imploded, sending wood and takeaway containers splashing leftover sauce and food across the apartment.

Thomas got hold of Raymond's arm and pulled it up behind his back. The sour acrid stench that wafted off of Raymond caused Thomas's eyes to water.

"What are you doing here?" Thomas demanded.

The light burst to life, blinding Thomas momentarily and giving the intruder enough time to flip him off his back and throw him across the room.

"What th—Thomas! Raymond?" Rochelle stood dressed only in a T-shirt.

Thomas stumbled to his feet and moved toward Rochelle who was standing at the entrance to the short passage.

"What in the hell is going on? Are you okay?" she asked.

Thomas nodded, then pushed her behind him. She tried to resist and work her way past him, but he spread his legs and stood his ground.

Raymond dusted polystyrene and leftover chips off his black jacket.

"For fuck's sake, Sis. Seriously! With so many white blokes around, you had to bed this thing?"

Thomas pushed Rochelle back when she made to rush at her brother. "That doesn't explain what you're doing in her apartment, Raymond."

"*Shurrup* you *blerrie coolie* half-breed." He pointed a shaking finger at Thomas. Then he leaned forward to catch Rochelle's eyes in a gap beneath Thomas's outstretched arms. "Where is it, Shelly?"

"Don't call me that!"

"You're lucky it's not *whore*. Now where the hell is that *bliksemse* envelope of Pa's? I know he kept it in the safe. I saw it every time he took out his rifle." He slinked past the rubble on the floor.

"Why are you so interested in it?" Thomas said as he struggled to keep Rochelle behind him. If it was money Raymond needed, why the envelope and not goods he could flog for cash? "Are you involved in the syndicate?"

Rochelle made to push past again, but he stepped back to force her into the passageway.

"Nothing to do with you, *ghamie*."

"Raymond, why did you hurt Pa? And what do you have to do with the envelope?" Rochelle called over Thomas's shoulder. "Dammit, let me pass!"

"No!" Thomas commanded.

"Pa? What happened to Pa?" Raymond stumbled.

"Raymond, Pa was attacked, hit over the head. He's lying in ICU on life-support for God's sake!" Rochelle's fingers squeezed the flesh of Thomas arms as her voice cut across the room.

Thomas watched as Raymond paled and his eyes enlarged to the size of the bottom of a wine bottle. "I told the bastards no one was to get hurt! Wasn't me. I swear it on Ma's grave."

"If you told whoever did that to Pa, about the safe, then dearest brother, you are guilty!" Rochelle's anger burned like a bonfire on a winter's night against Thomas's back. "Who was it? Because they were rather specific in their search, Raymond. And why the hell do you want it?" Rochelle hopped on Thomas's back and pushed down on his shoulders like a clawing cat.

"Just give it to me," his tone screamed desperation. Raymond was scared out of his wits. Whoever had paid him for the information was clearly a threat.

He steadied himself and stepped toward them. "I want that *blerrie* information now!"

Thomas readied himself for a showdown. Raymond hadn't come armed, and that was a relief.

"Neither of you have any idea who you're dealing with. You think I'm dangerous. The bloke who wants it will stop at nothing. Nothing, you hear me?"

A siren outside the apartment drew their attention, and Raymond took the gap to escape through her open front door.

Thomas stepped forward, allowing Rochelle to push past. "What the heck, Thomas?" she asked.

"If I'd let you pass, you'd have gone for him, and things would have ended badly. Don't deny it."

A glint on the floor caught his eye. He made his way past a fuming Rochelle. Kneeling he pushed away the debris from the destroyed coffee table to find a set of keys. He stood and held them up.

"Are these your . . .?"

"My keys! But not my . . . *mother fudger*!" Rochelle leaped across the room and grabbed the bunch of silver clanging keys.

"How did he? What the . . ." Rochelle squinted. "No way!"

"What?" Thomas walked to the kitchen.

"I remember someone, and only because the guy reeked of cat wee, the kind the CAT users smell of. It was a man in a hoodie who fell onto me one morning in the ED. The nurses had to pull him off, but then he ran. Could that have been Raymond?"

"Right now, I'd put nothing past that . . . your brother." Thomas opened the broom cupboard and took out what he needed.

"Someone found my keys at the reception desk later on that day. Said a patient found them out on the pavement and handed them in. Look," she said, picking up her bunch from her sideboard. "They still have that sticky stuff on them."

"He must have taken an impression to have this set cut."

"But how did he clone the toggle?"

"I reckon it's easy enough to slip in behind a resident who's entering the premises."

"Bloody arsehole!" Rochelle cursed as he began to clean up the mess. She stretched out her arm. "Here, let me help you."

She looked as cute as a nymph in her shirt. His T-shirt, now that he took a better look, and nothing else.

"Perhaps we should call the cops?"

"I don't think so. We'd have to tell them about the envelope and my gut says that's not a good idea." He began to sweep together the smaller bits of debris as she knelt and held the scoop for him.

"What about your friend?"

"It's one thing to ask for some protection but another entirely to ask him to keep this quiet." Thomas motioned toward the crushed table.

"Will you tell your superior officers tomorrow? You don't think they already knew Raymond was going to . . ."

"Nah, I just think they've found evidence of Ibrahim's involvement and they know he's my uncle. Seems the *skelm* old fool has gotten to your brother though." Thomas continued sweeping.

"That bastard. I knew he was up to no good, pretending to visit Pa and nosing around." Rochelle stomped her bare foot.

Thomas stopped sweeping and straightened himself. "I think your pa suspected it too. After tomorrow morning's meeting, I'll inform them about Raymond. Are you okay with that?"

"Yeah," she mumbled as she bent down and collected the larger pieces of her poor coffee table, the edge of the T-shirt lifting, giving Thomas a clear view of her ass. It took all his willpower not to take her there and then.

"Though I'd much prefer to get a hold of him myself and take to him with a *sjambok*!" She stood and looked toward him, her eyes on fire.

Thomas did not for one second doubt she'd beat the nonsense out of her criminal brother with a whip, not with the way the flames of Hades burned in her gaze at that moment.

"Best go lock that door and the security gate, then put on something a little less revealing?" Thomas wagged a finger toward front entrance.

The anger in her eyes faded as a mischievous smile spread across her face. Thomas groaned. She looked like a forest nymph with her mussed up multicolored tresses dangling over her shoulders.

Damn the open door!

"I don't think I should put on more clothes." She giggled and glided toward her front door. Placing a finger on it, she swung it closed before flipping the Yale lock and strutting toward him as she slowly pulled his T-shirt up and over her head. Her breasts sat plump and ready for the taking as her tongue glided along her lips, showing her hunger for him. His gaze followed her free hand as it dove down over her stomach and stroked the soft patch of hair between her thighs.

Only Rochelle Le Roux could shake what had just happened and find a way to upend every sane thought in his head.

19

"Lieutenant Campbell, Captain Mosele, and the rest of the intelligence personnel feel you're the best officer to analyze and decipher the information your father gathered," Rear Admiral Penlevan explained.

Thomas looked up at his superior. He had sat to the left of the man at the large oval table in the room now housing a full company of experts in various naval fields for the finalization of the training exercise.

"I would have thought you'd already verified and consolidated the information?" Thomas said respectfully.

"Permission to speak, Rear Admiral?" Captain Mosele stood from his chair.

"You're free to speak." Penlevan waved a hand and both men turned their stern gazes on Thomas, who tried not to feel like a grub on a mopane leaf, being served for dinner.

"The information has been verified, but it would seem your father was on the verge of cracking their means of communicating when he . . . ah . . . perished," the captain explained.

"Would they still be using this method after all these years?" Thomas was confused. Surely they'd have turned to more technological forms of comms.

"According to our investigations, the traffickers have become complacent in their dealings. Having not been caught for so long, they've not changed too many of their methods. Also, the older the technology used, the harder to track." Mosele explained.

"Okay, but wouldn't your communications specialist be the person for the job?" Thomas asked, looking down the table to a female officer around his age.

"Well, yes, but it seems your father was in the process of creating a key which would decipher their code. It's a code I've not been able to figure out." The female officer blushed and focused on her hands.

Mosele nodded. "Perhaps you should continue to explain, Lieutenant Samson."

"We need this key to unlock it?" Thomas asked. The relevance of his presence dawned on him. "You believe I have the key?"

"Yes," the female officer answered as she stood and made her way to where Thomas, the rear admiral, and the captain sat. "I believe your father's note is the key."

Thomas glanced at the manila folder, now neatly

inserted in a transparent plastic envelope. "Thomas's rhyme. And how does a simple children's rhyme work as a key?"

"Well I . . . we, were hoping you could help us?" she said.

Thomas closed his eyes as he drew in a deep breath, held it, then released it as he began to recite the words from the rhyme he'd dreamed a few nights before. "Monday's child . . ."

———

"Oooh! That's it!" Lieutenant Samson exclaimed as she leaned back from the blackboard now carrying all their scribbles and thoughts.

It was almost noon, and Thomas was concerned Rochelle might not wait much longer at the hospital. He'd sent her an SMS and asked if she was okay. He'd received a crazy smiley-face emoji as reply.

"We've cracked this a helluva lot sooner than I ever thought possible," Samson said, straightening her long body and placing her hands on her hips.

"My dad had already done more than half the ground work."

"Wow, I wish I could have met the man. From his notes, he comes across as quite the genius," she said as she penciled in the last digits of the longitude and latitude matching the key to the nursery rhyme his mother had taught him.

"Do you think it was a coincidence?" Samson asked.

"I don't know. But thinking back on the personality of my mother, as I've gleaned from her notes and diary entries, she was diabolical. Everything she did, she did for a reason."

Once they'd connected the sighting of the two boats, along with the information Thomas' father had already put together years before; figuring out how the rhyme worked as a key was easier. Everything else had fallen into place.

"How do you think he linked the rhyme to the syndicate?" she asked, looking up from her notes.

Thomas sat back and placed his steepled index fingers against his lips as his brain waded through the numerous pages of his parents' diaries. "I think I remember reading something." He reached to the pile of documents. "He wrote it down somewhere." Thomas searched through his father's papers sitting between them. "Ah, here it is." How had he not remembered this? "He'd begun to suspect a poem was being used as a way to convey their location and meeting times when he'd heard a few odd messages on the CB."

"You mean one of those Citizen Band radio's, like the truckers use?" Lieutenant Samson asked. "How did he know they used that form of comms?"

"Well according to his diary he was unable to find anything in any other form of communications until he saw his neighbors son playing with one and a light bulb flicked on. He also wrote here, on three occasions spanning over four months he happened upon three different channels, and each time a different line of Monday's Child was recited."

"So, your mother did teach you that rhyme for a reason!"

"Would seem so."

"Tell me he wrote down the channels?" Samson leaned over his arm to read the notes.

"He sure did. This, along with the key, will assist the Navy in bringing down the largest, longest-running syndicate of art thieves and human traffickers ever to exist." Thomas's chest swelled a little at the thought that after all this time, it was his father who would see Abad and his cronies rotting in jail.

"Do you still need my assistance?" Thomas asked as he gathered together all his notes and handed them over to Samson.

"No, I'll get this to Captain Mosele. I am sure our superiors will contact you should you be needed again."

"Nice to work with you." Thomas shook her hand, then left the room.

His first order of business was the barracks. He wanted to change. His favorite jeans and a comfortable polo should do it. His second was a phone call to the admiral's office, informing him of Raymond Le Roux's possible involvement in the human trafficking ring. He wasn't sure what good it would do, but all information was good information.

———

THOMAS LOOKS up into his rearview mirror, then over his shoulder as he reverses my four-by-four out of the parking lot at the hospital. His eyes find mine and my insides do flick-flacks. It's surreal, the effect this man has on me.

"Your pa doing better?" he asks, navigating the car onto the road.

"*Ja*, he's stable. It was eerie leaving the ICU with a cop standing guard outside though. "

"For now, it's safer that way," he puts his foot down on the accelerator and the pickup lurches forward and pushes in before a taxi who has no right of way.

"I hate taxi drivers. I wonder if the law will ever be able to catch up with them. They're rolling death traps."

"Last I heard, the police were too scared to touch them. Seems they carry more ammo than the army," I scoff.

"*Ja,* they're like the mob on wheels."

I think on Thomas's remark. It's so true. "The world truly has no idea how South Africa works, and that includes its minibus Taxi drivers. None of them have a valid license, their vehicles are unroadworthy, and the amount of accidents they cause with their cowboy driving ... Ugh, don't get me started."

"Ja-nee. I tell you, they're as corrupt as the government," Thomas adds.

"Where are we going?" I ask.

"I thought you deserved some fresh air, so I bought us a picnic basket over at Sollies Bazaar, and thought we'd go enjoy the view from my *stoep*?"

"Now that sounds like a plan. I predict that verandah's going to see many barbeques in the future," I say as I place my hand on his thigh.

"You know it." He winks at me.

I can't believe how hard I fought not to love this man! I really am a bloody nincompoop sometimes.

"I'm sorry about your coffee table, by the way. I thought we could head down to Weatherlys this weekend and I'll buy you a new one?"

His words, though sincere, remind me of Raymond's horrid intrusion. "Sure." I try to sound upbeat.

I don't want to discuss it any further and reach for the radio. My finger pushes the power button and my favorite station comes to life. An old song from the early nineties drifts out from the speakers. It's one of my favorite South African bands named after my favorite fruit, *Mango*. Claire Johnston's voice is haunting as she sings of "Moments" to her lover, and I let my thoughts drift back to last night—to Thomas and me. In my room. On my floor, and this morning in the shower, although that was ambitious. It's not built for two, but we made it work. My stomach flips at the thought of his mouth on my breasts and his fingers trailing down to my . . .

I need to calm these raging hormones. I push the black knob, and my window whines its way down. Mine is an old model Hilux. Everything squeaks and creaks, and goodness knows it goes like a bomb.

The wind flies in and whips my hair across my face.

"Do you have to go in to the base again tomorrow?" I look to Thomas, who's concentrating on the road.

"*Ja*, but it'll be the same as today. Up at sparrow's fart, but back early enough to be with you and your pa." He smiles.

God, I am the luckiest woman ever.

The southeasterly has pushed temperatures close to forty degrees Celsius and slaps my cheeks with its hot, blusterous squall. I squint into the wind as something in the side mirror catches my attention. *A green Nissan truck.*

I close the window and pull my fingers through the knots in my hair. "I swear I saw it parked outside the hospital," I mumble.

"What's that?" Thomas asks as he glances into the rearview mirror.

"Nothing." Ugh, my nerves are shot. There's obviously more than one of those on the roads. But I memorize the number plate just in case.

Thomas pulls my *bakkie* up to the front of the six-foot black iron security gate of his parents' house. He reaches into his pocket and pulls out a remote, then pushes the small yellow button on its belly. He sits back as we both wait for the large steel gate to roll open. At the same moment, I peer into the side mirror and again catch a green flash and the tail end of a green Nissan Nivara speeding up the road behind us. The hair on my neck stands on end.

"Do you think we've been followed?" I turn to look out the back window.

"The green Nivara? You're observant. Not sure. It drove past, and we should be okay once we're inside."

I know Thomas isn't as convinced as he sounds. His eyes dart back to the rearview mirror and his mouth does that thing, the pursed look that he does whenever he's worried or thinking. I don't put my thoughts into words, afraid if I verbalize the "but what happens when we leave here" then all hell will break loose.

He shifts the gear to first and we drive in. He stops and waits for the gate to close before pulling into the garage and switching off the engine.

20

I SPREAD THE PICNIC RUG THOMAS PURCHASED ALONG with the food out over the clay stone verandah, and place the basket on it as a sharp crack rumbles across the skies.

"Looks like a storm." Thomas's head arches back as he gaze out over the horizon.

We bring everything inside. I'm about to unpack the basket when Thomas's hand slips under my T-shirt and loosens my bra.

I let go of the bottle of chilled wine and turn, hopping into his arms before wrapping my legs around his waist as he plants delicate kisses along my jawline.

Thomas and I makes quick work of our clothes and I pull him back to rest between my open, inviting legs.

WHILE WE'VE NOT TOUCHED a crumb of the gorgeous delicacies Thomas bought, I can attest to a certain hunger of mine being satiated.

I roll us over and come to straddle him.

"Has anyone ever told you how beautiful you are?" His voice is low, like a lion's rumble at dawn.

"Many, but none with the love in their eyes that you have for me." I stroke his cheek with my index finger before I lean back as he arches up and slips back inside of me.

———

IT WAS a quiet drive back to the hospital. He suspected it was for no other reason except that for once, they were both content both in their hearts and souls. Their lovemaking had been rapturous, and Thomas prayed it'd never change.

With care, he turned the steering wheel and pulled into the hospital parking area.

"I'll be right behind you. I'm just going to throw away the leftovers," Thomas explained as Rochelle opened her door.

"Okay." She smiled, and planted a kiss on his lips. Not letting go of his cheek, Rochelle leaned back just enough to be able to look into his eyes. "I'm surprised we had time left to eat." She kissed him long and soft one last time before she slipped off her seat and made her way into the hospital.

Thomas's gaze caught movement in his rearview mirror. The green truck was back. It had followed them, he was sure. What were the chances there'd be one in the parking lot now, after one had driven behind them earlier?

He grabbed the bag of leftovers and disposable containers. His hunch gnawed at him. This was not a coincidence.

Thomas's eyes returned to the little mirror as the vehicle parked a few rows back.

He didn't want to alert the two passengers he was onto them. So, as naturally as he could manage, Thomas exited Rochelle's four-by-four, rubbish bag in hand, locked the door, and walked toward the hospital. At the entrance, he dumped the bag into the public trash can, and once inside, he pulled his phone out of his pocket and dialed 112. He couldn't bother his contact with this as well

"Hi, yes, look, I think a car's being stolen from the Simonsberg Hospital parking lot. Two men in a green Nissan Nivara, registration . . ." He turned and could only see half the registration plate from inside the foyer. He read it to the dispatcher and ended the call.

Hopefully that would buy them some time. He'd have to get himself and Rochelle safely to the base. He hoped *Oom* Derrek was in less danger.

Without drawing attention to himself, Thomas hurried through the foyer to the elevator as he sent a text to call in a favor of a different kind.

While the Navy had no jurisdiction on land, he hoped they'd afford him and Rochelle the protection from the syndicate they required. At least until the mission was completed and all the evildoers were behind bars.

Had the syndicate caught wind of their discovery?

He needed a plan A and B. This had been drilled into his head in the early days of his training.

Thomas stepped out of the elevator and made his way toward the ICU's waiting lounge.

He noted a different cop stood watch. Rochelle was still inside. He didn't want to alarm her. Not yet.

Thomas watched out the window of the waiting area, opposite the door to the ICU. He smiled as the spectacle below unfolded. Two police vehicles skidded to a halt behind the pickup. The passenger and driver doors swung open and two men exited, both with their arms in the air. The cops charged and pushed them up against the bonnet of their car.

One of two things could happen now. The police would realize this was a prank call or . . .

Thomas's grin broadened. Both were carrying weapons and obviously neither were licensed, because they were being cuffed and shoved into the back of a police wagon. The danger however, wasn't over.

Thomas's heart sank when he spotted another car —a black sedan which sped out of the parking area. It was obvious by the tinted windows and the way it had crawled past as the arrest was being made that they were the green Nivara's backup. He and Rochelle would have to hurry.

The door of the ICU opened behind Thomas. Rochelle stepped out, pale, tired, and worried. She sighed as she pulled the strap of her brown canvas handbag over her head.

"How's your pa?" Thomas asked.

An exhausted smile drifted across her face. "He's good. The tubes are out, and he is breathing on his own."

Thomas wrapped his arms around her. "Listen very carefully," he whispered into her ear.

Rochelle tried to pull away, but he held her firmly. "You need to follow my every move without question."

He felt her head nod against his chest.

Thomas cautiously navigated them toward the window, then told her what had transpired in the parking lot.

"Who do you think they are, and why are they after us?" Rochelle's whisper grew in a panicked crescendo.

"Shh." Thomas reminded her. "It's either my uncle or the syndicate. Either way, I think they're making a move for the documents your pa gave me. They're probably hoping I have no idea what they are, and that they're in my possession. Perhaps they've been watching the cops, thinking I'd hand any evidence in to them, instead of going to my superiors at the Navy."

"What about Pa?" Rochelle looked back toward the doors of the ICU.

"He'll be safe. I promise on my life. But I cannot leave you here. We need to get out of this hospital without being seen and to the base ASAP."

Rochelle nodded. "Why are we whispering?"

"Because I believe there are few people we can trust." He nodded toward the cop. "And the less anyone around us knows, the better."

"Why didn't they grab us at your house?"

Thomas thought about this. He did not like the logical conclusion to his thoughts. "I think they wanted to see if we had the papers. They probably . . ."

Rochelle's gasp echoed the disgust he felt. "They watched us?" Her whisper rose to a high-pitched exclamation.

"Shhh. I think they might be following us to see where I have stowed the documents."

Her cyan gaze had turned with the tide and now shone a dark moss-green, brimming with fear. She cupped his cheek, stood on her tiptoes and placed a kiss on his lips. "Let's go. Pa will be out for the count until morning."

21

"We need to get out of the hospital and into a taxi before we're spotted." Thomas held onto Rochelle's hand and the pair made their way to the foyer of the hospital.

Most ground floors of modern hospitals resembled a mall instead of a place where the ill and injured came for treatment. The area teemed with doctors, nurses, the affluent, and the not so wealthy. This hospital even sported a play area for small children.

Inside the coffee shop, waiters and waitresses scurried along serving the visitors and patients. A curio shop sat beside the coffee shop stocked with sedate cards of well-wishes and congratulatory gifts, snacks, sodas, bouquets, and clothes. Then came the pharmacy.

Thomas took the lead.

"What do you need in here?" Rochelle whispered.

"Cover. As much as I love that unruly fairy floss on your head, we need to hide it."

Thomas handed the teller a two-hundred rand note, and grabbed the shopping bag with one hand and Rochelle's with the other.

In a quiet corner behind the hustle and bustle of the shops, Thomas tucked the last few strands of Rochelle's hair beneath a baseball cap. It was quite a feat. Those wisps of blond, blue, and pink simply refused to be tamed, and snagged his fingers like the tentacles of an angry octopus.

Thomas slipped a cap onto his own and a pair of sunglasses down the front of his soft beige polo shirt, then nodded to Rochelle. "We need to get out of here without being seen."

"Follow me." She waved gripping his hand.

They made their way down some back stairs and into the belly of the hospital. A sharp musty smell drifted up his nose. The sudden silence jolted his eardrums and the world began to spin as disorientation set in. Thomas froze and looked around, trying to calm his sense of confused direction.

Rochelle squeezed his hand.

"This is the laundry, hence the smell." Rochelle explained as she tugged on his arm to get them moving.

Thomas's confusion began to settle as they made their way between bales of washing labeled in yellow and red tape. It was hot down here and smelled of, ugh, just nasty.

He followed Rochelle through a connecting door into an area with dim lighting. Pipes snaked along the low-hanging ceiling and the large water systems and generators churned and whined.

"Do you know where we're going?" Thomas asked.

"I make it my business to know everything about the places I work in. It's something I learned in North Africa. Always familiarize yourself with your surroundings. You might one day need an escape route. I just never thought I'd actually ever have to use it here!"

They reached a door with large red letters spelling EXIT painted across it.

"No, don't touch it. It has an alarm. Only certain personnel have keys. And when we use them, it's noted on the system."

"Then how do we get out?"

Rochelle grinned. "Here." She pointed to a door not three feet from the locked EXIT.

"Huh?" The irony of an unlocked door a few feet away from a locked one didn't escape Thomas. So typical of South Africa.

She laughed. It was a good sound. "Smokers need a way out too, you know. It's either on the roof or down here."

"You smoke?" Thomas exclaimed.

"Shhhh! No. But some of the nurses do. I have

friends you know." Rochelle pushed the door open a crack, scanned what little she could see, then swung it open. "All clear."

Thomas stepped out and quickly slipped on the pair of sunglasses he'd bought in the pharmacy. Rochelle followed suit, reaching for hers in her handbag.

They stood out the back of the hospital.

"Get us through that gate and onto that alley, then I'll take it from there." Thomas pointed to the alleyway running along the outside of the fence of the hospital grounds.

They walk-jogged to the left corner of the large backyard.

"Here we go." She stopped and pointed to a gate leading onto a street.

"It's locked." Thomas pointed out.

"Do you have my car keys?" Rochelle cocked her hips in a bossy stance as she held out her hand. Thomas couldn't help but imagine her turquoise gaze burning like hot blue flames from behind her shades.

His blood boiled and the muscle between his legs stirred. Good Lord, was there anything about this woman which couldn't make him hunger for her? Adrenaline surged through his bloodstream. There wasn't time for this now, but he couldn't help himself as he reached out and pulled Rochelle into him. He cupped her neck and his lips devoured hers.

Rochelle's body arched, pushing the apex between

her legs against his very hard need for her. Every inch of him burned. Forcing himself, he let go.

"Yup." He stepped back and dug into his pockets before handing a dazed, plump-lipped Rochelle the bunch of keys, then looked around to see if anyone was coming.

"Well, okay then. From now on you'll always have to keep my keys hidden if that's how you're gonna answer me," she teased.

Rochelle placed one last peck on his lips, then fiddled with the keys until she spotted what she wanted and slipped it into the lock. Its silver arch clicked open, and Rochelle pulled it out and unbolted the gate.

The pair stepped through and Rochelle closed it.

"You have a key for every lock in this place?" Thomas asked.

She smiled as she tucked the keys into her back pocket. "Skeleton. And no, not everyone has one."

Of course they didn't. Thomas took her hand in his. His nerves were frayed, but it did nothing to temper his desire. When this was all over, he was sure as hell going to make an appointment to have *the* chat with *Oom* Derrek, then make this lily of the valley his once and for all.

Thomas leaned down and kissed her one last time. Her lips were like honey to a badger. Heaven and hell wrapped in one.

A distant siren brought him back to earth and he pulled away.

"One for the road." He smiled, then led them off to his arranged rendezvous point.

They ran to the corner just as the black sedan Thomas had spotted earlier skidded to a stop and reversed.

"Shit!" He spun them around, and they sprinted back toward the small gate they'd just come from.

"Who are they?" Rochelle called.

There was no time to think. The car was on their heels.

He mock-swerved toward the gate before dodging left. They sprinted up an alley and through the back door of a boutique clothing store.

"Here." He shoved his phone into her hands.

"No, what the hell, Thomas?"

Even as she said it, the owner of the small clothing store ran into the back room of her shop. "Who the *blerrie* hell are you?" the tall blonde screamed.

"There's no time. I must distract them. My pass key is 8895. In the messages is where you must meet Thabiso Ntebe."

The defiance in her eyes told Thomas this would be a hard sell.

"Please, Rochelle. He'll know what to do. I'll be okay. I swear." He wrapped his arms around her.

Rochelle seemed to fiddle with something behind

his back as she hugged him, then tucked her hands in his back pocket and squeezed.

"Wait for twenty minutes, then go." He placed a last kiss on her pursed lips before he turned and ran back out. This was his plan B. He'd draw them away so Rochelle could meet with the corporal. He'd get her to safety, and they could both alert his superiors. He hoped.

Thomas turned and sprinted out the back door of the small shop. His legs carried him down the alleyway and into the street where two gangsta-looking men the size of hippo's, dressed in too-tight black T-shirts and jeans stood mumbling at the open doors of their car.

"Hey *poophols* . . . looking for something?" Thomas called as he sprinted down the road. If he could make it to the main street, he might just have a chance at escape.

22

THE EARTH SHIFTS BENEATH MY FEET. THE AIR IN MY lungs freezes. I can't breathe. I lean with my back against the wall and bend over, placing my hands on my thighs as I gasp. My knees threaten mutiny, and it takes all my willpower not to crumple into a small ball and cry out for help.

"Well? You going to buy something, or do I need to call the cops?" The woman taps her stiletto heel on the white tiled floor.

"I—I'll buy something." I stand slowly, taking care to keep my hands flat against the wall for support. Small black flecks pop bubbles across my vision.

The words bring a smile to her glossy red lips. And I manage a slow, much-needed, exhale. I've bought myself a little bit of time while I gather my thoughts.

I want to laugh. I want to cry. What in the seven

hells is going on, and who the fuck were those guys chasing us?

"Well, you won't find any clothes out here, *Chicci*."

I focus on her face. This bottle-blonde has spent way too much time at the plastic surgeon. Her lips stick out like a guppy with an allergy. The skin on her cheeks is so tight, I swear if she smiled any wider her face would tear.

"Ah, yes. Something plain and simple?"

"Mmm." Her eyes travel the length of my body from crown to toe. "I'll need a deposit first. Too many of you jeans-and-tatters types waltz in here wasting my time."

Oh, for the love of all things holy. I slip my hand into my handbag.

"Here." I hand her a credit card at the same time as I grip Thomas's phone and tap in the pass code.

———

Two and half thousand rand later, I look like a bloody *Gautenger* on holiday. This is how people from up north, in the Gauteng province, love to dress when they're down here. A pair of lime-green, cotton yoga pants and a white cowl-neck top with beads—beads! A pair of beige ballet slippers, a veldt hat, and Sophia Loren shades.

The only thing that's good about the huge sun hat is it covers all my hair and half of my face. I drew the line at her wanting to replace my handbag with a leather bag as large as a whale, for the price of an entire month's rent.

Glancing down at the phone screen one last time I memorize Thomas's instructions.

I step out and walk up the road surveying the area. No black cars or dodgy blokes are following me. I turn left on Rigel Avenue and head toward the takeaway shop for the planned rendezvous with this Thabiso Ntebe fellow. The distant aroma of deep-fried food, which usually makes my mouth water, twists my stomach into a nauseated knot. I have no idea what this bloke looks like, only that I must send him a text after I've ordered him a double cheeseburger with chips and a strawberry milkshake.

It's so hard not to give into my fear and run. My legs ache from me forcing them to stroll and not sprint up the street. My heart walks a tightrope between panic and broken. Did those guys catch up with Thomas? Is he safe? Where the bloody heck is he? Who are those men? Would my attempt to track him work? My lungs spasm again. I stand and lean against the wall of a local bank. My vision blurs and my mind balks as I force it away from thoughts of horror and the unknown.

Pull yourself together, woman! You've been through worse.

I force myself to remember the day rebels attacked the clinic in Kabala. I've made it through scarier situations. But my heart throbs, spasms, and throbs again. *No, you haven't*, its racing beat screams out. I wasn't in love the last time my life was in peril. This is about more than me. This time, it's all about the man I love!

I finally reach my destination, knees wobbling and innards roiling. I walk into the takeaway and up to the counter. I place the order and pay. It's quiet, except for a guy sitting in the corner mucking around on his phone.

I take a seat at an open table and pull out Thomas's phone from my bag. My heart cracks, and tears burn the back of my eyes. His screensaver is a photo of us standing on the verandah of his parents' home in Fish Hoek.

I grip the phone and hold it to my chest as I beg, *Please, may we be allowed many more beautiful moments on that verandah.*

A single word echoes across my spazzed out mind. *Faith!*

I take a deep breath, then open my eyes and type in the key pass and tap on messages. I send Thabiso the thumbs up. I start when the man across from me rises and walks over to my table.

"Thabiso Ntebe," he says and sits down.

His dark eyes frighten me; they have no emotion, and burrow into me like black diamond drill-tips.

"Where is my lieutenant?"

"I—I don't—look, he gave me his phone. He told me . . ." Tears stream down my cheeks.

"You're his squeeze then?" His dark coffee complexion lights up with his eyes.

I take a proper look at the man. I sincerely hope he is not supposed to be protection of some sort. I judge his build to be as small as mine. He looks more like a behind-a-computer-screen kind of guy than a man of kick-ass action.

"His what? Um yes I am his . . . girlfriend."

"Where is he?" Thabiso leans back, arms folded.

"Order nineteen," the girl behind the counter calls.

"I think this might be for you?" I hand Thabiso the docket.

He collects the white container and the milkshake. Can I trust this man?

"*Nca*', thank you." His use of the slang word for nice brings a smile to my face. "You not eating?"

I give him a sideways glance. Is he playing for time? "At a moment like this? Look," I begin as Thabiso pulls the food toward him and digs in. "Why did I have to meet you here?"

Thabiso swallows. "Lieutenant Campbell sent me an SOS. I did what he asked, so where is he?"

"What did he ask you?"

"Didn't you read the message?" He wipes his mouth with the back of his hand.

"Not all of them, no."

"First." He wipes his mouth, and turns his coal-black gaze on to me. "Where is my lieutenant?"

"Why should I trust you?" I swallow my tears, lean

back, and allow my eyes to scan the area for a quick
escape should I need one.

"You have no reason to trust me, but know this. I
was a throwaway. A half-breed bastard without
parents. Just like my lieutenant, my aunty didn't want
me. I was another mouth to feed and a body to clothe.
A reminder of what her sister was—a woman who'd
whored herself out to the Nigerians, got pregnant, then
died from AIDS. I was fortunate enough to escape the
scourge. I came out healthy and whole. By the time I
met the lieutenant, I was a grade-ten dropout who
would probably not have seen my eighteenth birthday.
That man, he saw something in me. The something I
still battle to see some days. He showed me how to pick
myself up out of the gutter, to stop blaming others for
my circumstances, and understand I am responsible
for me. If it weren't for him, I'd be dead. Another
statistic forgotten in a pile of paperwork on some dusty
shelf."

I can no longer fight back my tears. Sweet heavens,
how did I, me, Rochelle, land a man like Thomas only
to hand him to crooks she's certain will harm him once
they discover he no longer has the papers on him.

"I . . . I don't know." I reach into my handbag and
grab the overused tissue from the hospital, wipe my
eyes and nose and say, "We were being pursued. He left
me, gave me his phone, told me to come here."

I watch as Thabiso slurps the last of his shake and
wipes his mouth, this time he uses the flimsy serviette.

"He acted as a diversion? Not sure how we'll find him. I need to get you to safety first."

I hold up my hand to indicate I was going nowhere. "I have a mini GPS tracker. I bought it after I thought I'd lost my keys. Anyway, I slipped it into his pocket."

"Not just a pretty face, *neh*!" He nods then takes another deep slurp of his milkshake.

Ugh. I roll my eyes. If I had a gold coin for every time a man said that to me.

"Did he tell you?" I need to know how deep this young man has been drawn into this mess.

"About his parents? Only some."

"Okay, so we can find his location. Do we go to where they're holding him and just tell them he's already handed the information over to the Navy?" A thousand and one questions tumble around inside my head.

"*Hayibo, Sissi.* Just calm down, and no. We tell those *skebengas* nothing!" He tries to calm me, but his reminder that we're dealing with criminals only makes it worse.

"Why? It's obvious they must be after those documents."

Thabiso shakes his head. "Let me help you understand how these people work. Two years ago, while on a training mission, we came across a merchant boat attacked and left to rot by pirates."

I feel my eyebrow arch. "Pirates?"

"Yup, real-life *tsotsis* of the ocean, minus the parrot and the eye patch."

I can't help but chuckle at Thabiso. I've never heard anyone associate the word *tsotsi* with a pirate. It's usually used to name thugs and criminals, which I guess pirates are.

"Anyway. It was an ugly sight we found on that limping vessel. There was one survivor, who'd managed to hide and escape the massacre. Poor man told us a story of horror. They hadn't put up any resistance. They'd given the fools what they wanted as the cargo was insured and not worth their lives. But as it turned out, it wasn't only the cargo they were after but blood also. My point? If these men who were chasing you and my lieutenant get their hands on you, they'll kill you both anyway. To tie up loose ends and all."

Thabiso's tale turns my smile upside down and runs cold water down my back.

He looks over his shoulder into the street. "They'll keep you alive until they have you both and the information, so we have some time. That said, give me your phones."

My back straightens, and I grab onto my handbag.

"It's very easy to track cell phones these days, so please, hand them over." He stretches out an open hand and I reluctantly give him both devices. But before I let go of them, I say, "My pa . . ."

"He's in good hands. I promise."

Something in this young man's voice garners my trust and I comply.

"Okay, here's what needs to happen." He shifts the empty containers out of the way and begins to pull the cell phones apart.

23

It didn't take them long to find Thomas. Two against one—he would have stood a chance if number one, now sporting a broken tooth and bloodied nose thanks to a left foot in the gob, hadn't cheated and pulled out his taser.

His nerve endings twitched and jumped as they bound his hands behind his back, taped his mouth, and pulled a sack over his head. One of the two fat smelly bastards threw him, bound and gagged, on the back seat of the car. Thankfully, Thomas hadn't wet himself from the shock. He stilled his breathing, which wasn't easy considering the remaining joules running rampant in his body. Using what senses he could, he tried to orientate himself. His hearing was the most important. They were passing fewer cars and he'd heard children's voices once or twice, which indicated they were in the suburbs. This was good, it meant they weren't going to kill him and dump his body in the veldt – yet.

It felt like an eternity before the car hobbled over what he suspected was the sidewalk and pulled into a driveway.

"You fools! Anyone can see you!" a familiar voice whispered into the window.

"But the windows are tinted," Tweedledee's voice murmured.

"I'll open the garage. Pull in there."

A glacier settled in the pit of Thomas's stomach. It *was* Ibrahim who sat behind all the duplicity. He'd know that voice anywhere. Why was he shocked?

He'd seen his uncle's dark side many times growing up, but a part of him had always hoped there was a little light too.

The rolling of a metal door told Thomas the garage was opening. The car glided into the safety of its dark belly and the door closed. Thomas was unceremoniously yanked out of the back seat and the sack ripped off his head. The tape stayed in place.

"Well, well, what do we have here?" Ibrahim sniggered.

Thomas fought against his restraints. More than anything, he wanted to wrap his hands around the man's throat and throttle the smirk off his self-righteous face.

"Why'd you have to make things so complicated, Thomas? If you'd just followed the rules and given me what was mine, none of us would be here now." Ibrahim rubbed his index finger and thumb across his moustache and down his beard as he considered Thomas.

"While I've never been fond of disciplining those who don't obey, I've looked forward to the day I could put you back in your half-breed place. And just like your whore of a mother, you like *kaffirs*. You blaspheme upon the name of your creator by choosing the infidel above your own people. Ah, but then I suppose one cannot blame you. You are not pure."

For fuck's sake, the man loved the sound of his own voice.

"You are but half of the goodness of your people and half of the scum—the scourge which has populated this earth. A bastard. A nothingness. But soon, we will find your white slut. I will have those documents. Oh yes, I know he gave them to you. If I'd known sooner that Henry had delivered them to Derrek, you might not have been here today. Le Roux did a good job of pretending he'd had everything destroyed or sold."

It was Ibrahim who'd had Rochelle's Pa harmed.

A memory from a night where a little boy's world had come to a crashing, horrendous end, flashed through Thomas's mind. White-hot anger overrode all common sense. Images flashed across his mind's eye from that night when he'd sat helplessly in the back seat of his parents' car, replaying like a bad movie. The gunshots, the screaming, and the blood. Blood which Ibrahim had seen fit to spill.

Thomas moved, too quick for Tweedledee or Dum to realize what he was doing. His forehead came crashing down on his uncle's nose. Stars and sparks blurred his vision as a yowl of pain erupted from Ibrahim's mouth and blood spattered across the garage. The two security scums jumped to life.

One grabbed the muscles running from his neck to his shoulder, digging hard fingers into his skin and jerking him back as the other pummeled his fist into Thomas's belly.

Ibrahim stumbled back, a hand over his bleeding nose.

"Stop!" His nasal exclamation brought his rabid dogs to halt.

"Take him to the study. Make sure he can't move." He pointed a shaking blood- and saliva-soaked finger at Thomas. "You'll pay for that, boy. You'll pay for everything!"

Thomas allowed one of the fat blokes, who reeked of curry masala and tobacco, to push him forward and steer him toward the study. He could only pray Thabiso and Rochelle had found one another, and Rochelle was safely on her way to the base. If he could make sure she remained out of Ibrahim's grasp, half the battle was won.

Tweedledee pulled out an old wooden chair which stood in the corner of the room and shoved Thomas onto it. Using plastic tie-downs, he strapped Thomas's ankles to the front legs and his bound wrists to the crest rails of the backrest, while Dum scanned outside the windows. He made sure to land a solid punch across Thomas's jaw before he walked out, his clone in tow, and closed the door behind him.

Searing, hot anger rushed through Thomas's veins and clouded his judgment. Ibrahim was the instigator of all the heartbreak in his life. The man who, with a single wave of his crooked hand, had stolen his family and now threatened the only person he loved. When this was over, he'd see Ibrahim locked up and the keys thrown into the deepest, darkest canyon on this earth.

The wave of adrenaline which had washed over him earlier ebbed, and Thomas slouched. He had to find a way out of this. The chair wobbled and pulled him from his slump. If memory served, this was the antique which was never all that sturdy. If he could lift himself and the chair up, then sit down hard enough, he was sure something would give. About to give his plan a try, voices in the passageway told him Ibrahim was returning.

Thomas braced himself. He'd have to listen to more of the fool's sodded gloating. The door swung open just as Thomas's back pocket vibrated.

24

"ALL RIGHT, I'VE PINGED HIS LOCATION."

Relief replenishes my exhausted adrenal glands as I watch Thabiso scribble down an address. It's taken the genius an hour to crack the small GPS I slipped into Thomas's back pocket. It would've have taken less had he not destroyed my phone, but the man was adamant this was the safer route to follow.

I look back at the screen. The road's name looks familiar.

"Is that Glen Road?" I point to the screen of his phone, still amazed at what this guy achieved without a computer.

"*Yebo*, yes."

I smile at his use of the Zulu word, and a phrase made popular by cell-phone advertising. "No way. Shit, shit, shit! This can't be!" I slap a hand over my mouth when the handful of customers in the joint turn their heads in my direction.

"What's wrong?" he whispers.

"That's Ibrahim Abad's house!" I point a shaky finger to the flashing red dot on his cell-phone screen.

"*Hayibo*! You mean the same Ibrahim Abad who's sat on the council for the last three decades?" He clicks his tongue and shakes his head.

"One and the bloody same."

He leans back into his chair and folds his arms across his chest. "Right then, we'll need some backup."

"Fair enough, but how will we convince the police, without proof, that Ibrahim is holding his nephew against his will?" My knees shake, and I am about to spew the contents of the picnic I shared earlier with Thomas.

Thabiso leans toward me. "Listen carefully . . ."

———

I FOLLOW Thabiso and the tall woman he introduced as Thomas' secretary down the sidewalk.

"You can trust Janet I promise. She has connections, as well as the Captains ear." Thabiso reassures me.

We arrive at the entrance of our destination.

I give the tall brunette another once over. Thomas had mentioned her once or twice. I knew she ran his office and they were friends outside of work, but I had no idea she was so beautiful. I swallow back the taste of jealousy souring my taste buds.

"Come we don't have time to waste." She commands, the places a hand on my shoulder, "It's Thomas who should worry. Luckily I don't date my *tjommies* girlfriends." She winks and steps inside, her stilettos clicking a hurried staccato down the hallway as I'm left gaping like a guppy.

Thabiso grins and shakes his head waving a hand for me to enter first.

"Will he listen to us?" I ask stepping inside the building on the naval-training base.

My heart hasn't stopped pounding since Thomas left me in the Boutique.

"Yes. Captain Van Staden is a genuine bloke. He takes care of his own. If he listens to us, you can be damn sure he'll get the big *amakhosi* to act as well." Janet looks back over her shoulder to me as we make our way to the base commander's office.

"Do you know who it was that Thomas gave the information to here at the base?" I ask, somewhat out of breath as we make our way to the office.

"*Aikona*." Thabiso shakes his head. "That information is beyond my security clearance, but Captain Van Staden is the CO of the training base and he will know."

———

THE TALL, lanky man with a grey crew-cut and a moustache, strides back into his office where he left us a few short minutes ago to contact the rear admiral. He reminds me of the wing commander in that fighter-pilot movie from the eighties.

He comes to sit down behind his desk and places his chin on his steepled hands. "I've informed Rear Admiral Penlevan of your predicament. His thoughts echo mine. I may share some of what Thomas has been collaborating on with you, in order to garner a clearer point of view on the situation."

I look at Thabiso and Janet then back to the captain who skewers us both with dark grey stares.

"What I tell you here may never leave this room. In fact, my secretary will shortly arrive with nondisclosure documents for you both to sign."

I nod. *Just get on with it,* I plead silently.

"It seems the information Thomas had attained is vital evidence which will enable the Navy to bring down a ring of human and antiquity art traffickers."

I lean back in my chair. "This I already know."

The captain eyes me, pressing his lips together until they blanche, then continues. "We'll have to involve local law enforcement." He holds up his hand to stop my protestations at the same time as Janet comes to stand behind me and places a hand on my shoulder.

"Just listen," Her voice is strong yet calming, I can understand why she and Thomas are good friends.

Captain Van Staden sighs, "I share your concerns about there being corrupt members, but the rear admiral has assured me they are certain the group of men and woman currently collaborating with them are trustworthy. Also, this will be a coordinated mission, both on land and at sea."

"Why?" I shift closer to the edge of my seat.

"I beg your pardon?" The captain looks ruffled.

Janet squeezes my shoulder, but I don't care.

"Why use the police at all? You have an entire fleet at your command!" My voice snaps around the words.

The man's eyebrow cocks as he considers my frazzled form. "Because, Doctor Le Roux, we are the South African Navy and, according to international law, no defense force is allowed to act within its own borders. Thomas's kidnapping is a local law enforcement matter."

I can't sit still. Imaginary ants crawl up my back and legs. "So, what? We just leave Thomas to the mercy of potentially corrupt cops?"

"Yes and no. There is a small loophole we can use as a work-around. So, if you would, please calm down."

Thabiso sits as still as a concrete block beside me. He's not so much as uttered a word.

"And what is this loophole?" I push.

"We can make it look as though Lieutenant Campbell went AWOL."

"But he's been kidnapped!" I try not to scream at the man.

Thabiso shifts uncomfortably in his eat as he addresses the captain. "Permission to speak, Captain?"

"You are in civilian clothing, seaman; no need to ask permission." Captain Van Staden nods.

Thabiso directs my attention toward him. "If they report the lieutenant AWOL, they are able to attach a unit of military police to the team going after Ibrahim."

"This will solve our problem of potential corrupt officers and give us the ability to attend to the lieutenant immediately," the Captain finishes and stands. He gazes out of his window before turning to face Thabiso as I digest this revelation.

"And what is your part in this whole mess, Seaman?"

"I received an SMS from the lieutenant earlier today, but as you can see, I arrived too late."

"And why hadn't he come to me?" Captain Van Staden asks as he returns to his seat behind the large desk.

I look up, swallowing the nausea slowly threatening to wreak havoc with my body. "He wanted to get us to the safety of the base before he contacted anyone. We weren't sure who was after us." It's the only explanation I can offer.

The captain nods. I can see the resignation and understanding in his grey eyes. "Well, let's first get our lieutenant back safely, and then we'll take it from there." Captain Van Staden leans back in his chair. I can see the cogs of his well-honed military mind turn.

"Great. Who do I go with?"

"Doctor Le Roux, this is not a trip to the movies."

I jump to my feet. "I have been chased by thugs, and my father's been beaten within an inch of his life, not to mention surviving three years as a doctor in the pits of Africa. Living day in and day out with the constant threat of a guerilla army wanting to take over is a danger I am familiar with. I am coming along!"

Janet comes to stand beside me, arms folded and an aura that shouts out like an angry neon sign – Women's power.

The captain considers her then returns his focus to me. He rubs the bridge of his nose with his forefinger. "On any other day, I'd have you thrown into the brig, but I can see that would cost me more trouble than it's worth. Fine, come along. But you'll remain in the vehicle at all times, Doctor Le Roux. As for you Janet, there's paper work you'll need to deal with." The captains icy gaze tells me that's as much leeway as he is willing to give me.

Janet nods once then faces me, "It's gonna be fine. You're in great hands." She wraps her arms around me in a warm embrace then leaves.

25

THE WAFT OF CURRY AND TOBACCO ASSAILED THOMAS'S nostrils as Ibrahim's ogre landed another punch in his gut. It twisted and dented the muscles protecting his innards. Thank fuck for Drill Sergeant Masingo. Those ten sets of one hundred sit-ups every PT session were what kept his shit together right now.

"Do you honestly think I like to see you hurt?" Ibrahim's voice tripped across the room to where Thomas sat.

Thomas looked up and smiled. "Of course you do. I'm the scourge that soils your world. But before you get your gorilla to aim another dirty shot, answer me this. Why my parents?" Thomas knew why, but he wanted to hear it from the bastard's mouth.

Ibrahim's shoulders squared as he made his way toward Thomas and leaned down so his swollen face sat inches from his own. "Your mother was a whore.

She disgraced our family name, and your father . . ." he straightened, ". . . was the man who tainted her."

Hatred burned in the bottom of Thomas's stomach. But he kept his face straight. Never again would he give his uncle the satisfaction of seeing him affected by his anger. "Was that the only reason you murdered them?"

The man's face had turned a nasty shade of grey at the same moment as his eyes narrowed to two dark slits on his face. "Your father made it his business to see me ruined."

"So, you shot your own sister and her husband! Your own blood! You, who bows his brow to his god of so-called love and righteousness every day, wears the blood of his own family on his hands like a pair of tainted gloves! You are the *kaffir,* Ibrahim!"

Ibrahim turned away from him, but not before Thomas caught the fear and shame in the old man's eyes.

"Where's the evidence your father collected, Thomas?" Ibrahim returned to his former line of questioning as he nodded to the muscle.

Tweedledum's flat hand connected with Thomas's cheek. A loud *thwack* echoed across the room and shook Thomas's grey matter.

Shit!

When he got out of these bonds, payback would be the last of this fat oaf's problems, Thomas spat a glob of red saliva onto his uncle's carpet.

"What did you do with the folder Le Roux gave you?" Ibrahim shouted from across the room before the oaf's hand connected with his cheekbone a second time.

Thomas's brain thudded against his skull and his vision blurred. How much longer could he withstand the assault? Blond fairy floss hair drifted past his vision. "Rochelle . . ."

"What was that?" Ibrahim hurried toward him and lifted his chin.

"*Jou ma se . . .*" He didn't get to finish his curse as Ibrahim knocked the side of his face with something hard, and the world went black.

———

THOMAS'S VISION CLEARED. How long had he been here? Hours? Days? It felt like forever.

The slightest movement outside the window at the back of Ibrahim's study caught his eye.

Thank you, Thabiso!

Thomas lifted his head and gave his uncle the most arrogant, *I'm gonna kick your filthy ass* look he could conjure.

Ibrahim frowned, scrutinizing his nephew. Milliseconds before the synapses in his rotten brain could put two and two together, Thomas gathered all of his remaining strength, lifted the chair, and sat down hard. The old. rickety wood cracked and snapped just as the window and the study door burst like exploding pomegranates.

Ibrahim fell to the floor, yelling as his hired muscle tried to dash for the door, but was summarily knocked down and cuffed.

Men clad in black tactical gear somersaulted through the openings, aiming large automatic rifles at all of them.

Thomas pulled his hands and legs free of the broken chair.

"Lieutenant Thomas Campbell?" a man in black bulletproof overalls, helmet, and mask asked.

"Yes."

"Please come with me." The man knelt and opened a knife cutting through Thomas's bonds.

Thomas stumbled to his feet. The officer leaned over to remove what was left of the tie-downs and chair still strapped to him. The passageway was quiet, and the front door still intact. They'd obviously pushed their way in once his auntie had answered the door. In doing so, they'd given Ibrahim and his thugs little notice of their presence.

Outside, his auntie wailed and waved her arms as she was pushed into the back seat of a police wagon. Neighbors peered out their front doors, and passing cars slowed to get a glimpse of the drama unfolding in the peaceful neighborhood.

Thomas squinted through his swollen vision. Beyond the gate stood a civilian vehicle. The door opened, and Rochelle jumped out from the front seat.

"What the . . .?"

"Thomas!" she yelped and pulled free of the officer who tried his darnedest to hold her back. She sprinted toward Thomas. Relief, gratitude, and utter exhaustion washed over him.

"Oh, Thomas, are you okay? What has that asshole done?" She wrapped her arms around his neck, threatening to cut off his air supply, then pushed back and began to inspect his injuries.

"Seaman Ntebe!" he greeted the young corporal who was hot on her heels.

"Sir."

Thomas stuck out his hand. "Thank you for taking care of her and thanks for saving my arse."

"All good, sir. But you owe Janet big time." He grabbed Thomas's hand as the police led Dum and Dee out of the house, followed by Ibrahim.

"She got you in to See Van Staden?" Thomas smiles.

"Yebo, Yes." Thabiso nods as the an irate voice drew their attention.

"You can't do this! Do you know who I am? Thomas! Thomas, tell these men they're playing with fire!"

Thomas glared at the man who'd killed his parents and put the woman he loved in danger. "I think you will find a safe beneath the back stairs of the house.

The code is my auntie's birth date. Inside will be all you need to throw this man away."

"How do you . . .?" Ibrahim shook two bound hands out in front of him.

Thomas stepped toward Ibrahim. "You forget. I might have been a quiet boy, but I always watched. After every meeting, you would put things in that safe. You never saw me. And I am sure after all these years, you've never changed your ways."

His uncle's olive cheeks and brown lips turned bright red. "You infidel! You bastard!" he screamed.

"No, uncle, the only bastard here is you. You killed my parents. I remember it now as clear as the rain which poured down on us that night. It was you who pulled the trigger!"

"Prove it!"

"Oh, I'm sure your two clowns will offer up all the evidence needed to keep their asses safe in prison." Thomas fought back the urge to connect his fist with his uncle's jawbone. He was better than that.

Turning to join Rochelle, life suddenly slowed down. Thomas watched as Ibrahim lurched forward and grabbed the side arm of an unsuspecting constable. He ripped and tugged, kicking the poor policeman as he freed the weapon from its leather holster.

"Weapon!" someone screamed.

Thomas reached for Rochelle, wanting to pull her behind him for safety.

"Thomas!" Rochelle twisted out of his grip as her

voice echoed off the brick walls of the house a split second before a shot thundered across the sky.

Thomas made to push her behind him, but Rochelle was too quick for him and stepped between him and Ibrahim.

The tactical officer threw himself onto Ibrahim as a crack split through the air. Rochelle crumpled to the ground.

"Rochelle!" Thomas fell to his knees then crawled toward her.

Blood seeped through her lime-green outfit and pooled around her in the brick walkway. Thomas desperately pressed one hand against her abdomen as he wrapped the other around her limp body and pulled her to him.

No, this couldn't be. Not now. The bad guys had been caught, and they were meant to be together forever! His index finger slipped up toward her neck and fumbled for a pulse . . .

26

THOMAS AND I CLIMB THE GREY GRANITE STEPS LEADING to the large entrance of the museum. It's taken almost five months, a wedding, and the recovery from a gunshot to get here. We are in Cairo, Egypt. The journey is both for our honeymoon and to return the exquisite artefact taken from Ibrahim's study.

A short man, with a decent-sized potbelly and a full head of white hair to match his bushy moustache, waits for us at the large entrance.

"Good day. Professor Frood?" Thomas asks as he holds out his hand in greeting.

"*As-salāmu ʿalaykum*. You must be Lieutenant and Doctor Campbell?" The plump grey haired man greets.

"It's just Thomas, please. I'm no longer a navy man." Thomas explains as they shake hands.

"Ah yes. I heard whispers you were to follow in your father's footsteps. The world needs more people who care about the vulnerable and stolen histories of war torn countries." He lets go of Thomas hand and takes mine proffering a warm smile. "Follow me."

I follow the two men inside but find it hard to concentrate on the conversation between Thomas and the professor as we walk past the exhibitions. The museum is vast and filled with all the wonders of ancient and modern Egypt. My brain battles to comprehend the riches and beauty of it all.

The muscle on the left side of my abdomen aches a little from the drop in temperature. The bullet had miraculously missed all my vital organs and arteries. It was what we call a through-and-through. Only flesh and skin were torn as the projectile sliced into me.

I'd been discharged along with Pa a week after being shot, and Thomas had been granted compassionate leave to take care of the both of us for another week.

Not long after that, Thomas proposed beneath the tree he'd first kissed me. And if life had taught us anything it was the simple fact that it waited for no one. With no reason to prolong the inevitable, we tied the knot. It was sublime. I wore Ma's wedding dress, with a few adjustments here and there. Thomas stood proud in his gorgeous navy formals. Janet stood beside Thomas as best man, and Grace my maid of honor with Thabiso making a very proud and rather funny master of ceremonies.

We got married at dusk in the vineyard then celebrated throwing one helluva party afterwards with Pa and our friends. Now here we are, in glorious Egypt.

Thomas and I follow the professor up and down stairs and through passageways until we reach a large, dusty office.

"I was told you were part of the team who broke the ring of smugglers and not only saved this treasure, but also the lives of many children?" The professor's words draw me back to the conversation.

"Well, it took more than me, but yes." Thomas nods and smiles.

"And the kingpin was your uncle?"

Thomas lowers his head. "Of sorts, yes."

"I understand your shame. But I have never believed we should carry the blame for the wicked actions of others." The professor pats a hand on Thomas's back.

"If it helps," I intervene, "Ibrahim is in a world of trouble, stuck in jail with no hope of being let out on bail. He will pay the price for the harm and destruction he has caused so many. Sadly, though many were arrested or detained, the true head of the snake has still managed to elude authorities. While they've stifled the trafficking out of South Africa for now, Ibrahim was not the mastermind behind it all, but only a cog in a much larger machine."

"This is both sad and good." Professor Frood shakes his head.

"But I promise to find the true offender and bring him to justice." Thomas says.

"Ah, so you will make it your work to finally track down and end this tyrannical trade?" A bright smile spreads across the professors face.

"I hope to." Thomas swings the bag off his shoulder and zips it open.

Gooseflesh peppers my arms and neck. From the bag, he pulls out a box and places it gently on the table before us. It's unreal to think we have been given the privilege of returning this exquisite scepter to its rightful resting place.

I watch as the old Egyptian man pulls on a pair of white cotton gloves and removes the lid. He lifts the yellow cotton and gasps.

"In all my life, I had never thought I would ever lay my eyes on this, the *Sekhem* scepter, again."

With great care, he lifts the polished artifact out of its secure cradle, and I marvel at the brilliant luminescence within its intricate carvings. His dark amber eyes stretch wide and light up like a streetlamp as he admires the paddle-like scepter.

"We also found it's provenance, stashed in Ibrahim's safe with a lot of other artifacts and their papers." Thomas hands over an envelope.

"May the gods bless you both. I thank you for returning to my people that which was taken." He graces us with eyes brimming with tears and a smile brighter than the sun.

———

"I GOT A CALL FROM PA," I say to Thomas as we stand on the deck of the boat.

"Is he alright?"

"Yeah. He's just gotten back from court." I sigh. Matters concerning my brother are always emotionally taxing.

"They found Raymond as high as a kite in some brothel. Apparently it didn't take much to get him to spill the beans on Ibrahim. His dealings have cost him six extra years. Unfortunately, the judge took pity on him after Pa spoke up. He'll be one of a select few to spend his time working on a rehabilitation farm somewhere in Namaqualand."

Thomas shakes his head as he hugs me. "Is Pa well enough to go back to work?"

"Try and stop him." I grin. "He looks forward to our return from honeymoon. But added we shouldn't rush on his account."

"Ja. I got an SMS from Thabiso wishing us well." Thomas unwraps his arms and stands beside me.

"He's a good man. We should invite him over for dinner when we're back."

A cool breeze lifts off the waters of the Nile, bringing with it both the good and not-so-good smells of Cairo.

"This is magical. I never thought we'd spend our honeymoon here on a beautiful revamped steamboat, like the one in that old detective novel." I take in the wonders.

"Minus the murders of course," Thomas replies, as he leans over the railing and gazes down at the murky waters of the Nile.

We'll spend a week cruising one of the world's greatest treasures.

On the horizon, the pyramids glow as the setting sun illuminates their ancient stones. Thomas shifts so he stands behind me and once more wraps his arms around my waist.

My eyes scan all the figures moving along the banks of the Nile. It is strewn with all sorts, from cattle, to camels, to women washing and children swimming.

"We are so very blessed," Thomas whispers into my ear.

"That we are, husband of my heart. That we are." And I turn to kiss him as we did the very first night we met.

THE END

AUTHOR'S NOTE

This story ended up very different to what it was originally planned to be. It is full of South Africanisms at their best, and worst.

The idea behind my story is to show the world that hatred and racism does not belong to a single race, but that every person, no matter the opportunities or lack thereof in their life, is responsible for their own actions. We cannot blame others for the way we think, act, or feel.

Also, I wanted to highlight the blatant corruption of the South African government, so kindly hidden by the mainstream media's misleading rhetoric.

Then lastly, I felt obligated to bring my readers' attention to the very real and ancient practice of human trafficking, and that it was not only the Empires of times past which practiced such an evil

trade. It is a practice which still runs rife on the
African continent today.

While this story is fiction, woven between the lines are
many truths; like the hill covered in white crosses.

The remark of a president building a huge home using
the money allocated for government housing also lays
claim to a truthful origin.

Then lastly.

Simons Town is a real city in the Cape province, but I
used a lot of creative license in my description of it.

I am sure you enjoyed the read.

Please feel free to reach out to me.

http://michelledaltonauthor.com

or

michelle@michelledaltonauthor.com

FORGET ME NOT

LOST & FOUND - BOOK TWO

Prelude

Queensland in February is like sitting in a sauna with all your clothes on.

Isabella Irish flapped her T-shirt to and fro, hoping to create some airflow and cool off. She came to stand beneath the blooming poinciana tree which created a canopy over the open-air stage. The popular Eumundi Markets were as crowded on a Wednesday as they were on Saturdays. It'd been months since she'd visited the busy Sunshine Coast bazaar. Her stall, which had showcased her art, had sat not too far from where she was now—before Mark had secured her first break.

Two men and three women stepped onto the stage and

positioned themselves with their traditional indigenous instruments.

The earthy Australian music drifted out of a didgeridoo and flowed through her body, the player's circular breathing imitating the rain and the wind in his songs of the earth and the sky.

A hand drum soon joined in and Issi found herself carried away to a distant place as she rode the rhythm and sound of the song.

The fog which always clouded her fractured cognizance lifted, and a clarity she had not experienced since the terrorist attack, seeped into her damaged brain. She closed her eyes and shut out the hustle and bustle around her, enjoying the brief reprieve from a mind which had lost so much.

A deep bassy tone emanated from the instrument as the player worked the mouthpiece with his breath. The sound painted a picture of the elements, and kangaroos hopping across a vista—*boing, boing*. A third instrument joined in, adding a crispness like dry grass brushed by the wind . . . It drew her away from the present and into an open space of land, her heart echoing the beat of the drum. Reds and golds unfurled around her. The music drew her back to an ancient time . . .

"Hey. You enjoying the music?" Jeff leaned in with his chin on her shoulder.

"Geez!" Issi slapped a hand to her chest as she jumped.

"Sorry, lovely." He proffered a handsome smile along with his apology.

"Yeah. It tells a story if you listen closely." She returned the gesture to show him she was okay. "Where's Sam?" She leaned past Jeff. "I can't see him," she asked her ridiculously tall friend.

"Two rows down. He's discovered a stall that sells exotic food and art." Jeff rolled his eyes. "And I swear the stallholder's accent is just like yours."

"I don't have an accent." Issi waved off Jeff's odd comment. For a born-and-bred Australian, she sounded nothing like one. But her different way of pronouncing words, according to the specialist doctors, could be due to her acquired brain injury.

"Come. We need to save that man from himself. I can see him buying a truckload of foreign foods I know I won't eat. I mean, what in the holy heck is *paap*?" Jeff's lips tried to wrap themselves around the foreign word. The outcome was hilarious and Issi bit back her laughter.

He slipped an arm through hers and guided her to where Sam stood tasting food and peppering the short, plump stallholder with questions.

"Are you still tasting?" Jeff nudged his partner, who nodded and swallowed.

"This *pap* is good once you put some honey in it," he replied.

"What is it exactly?" Issi pointed to the bowl of what looked like bleached polenta.

"*Haai*. Why don't you know what pap is?" The woman's astonished expression caused Issi to pause.

Taking a step away from the table she shook her head.

"It's a maize porridge." Sam graciously drew the vendor's attention back to him. "Really, you both need to broaden your palatable horizons." He winked at Issi.

"*Ja*. So this is Achar," she said, glancing at Issi once or twice more. "And you can eat it with a lot of stuff, especially wif your *p-ah-p.*" She pronounced the word slowly. "It gives it this really *lekka* . . . erm, *wat is nou die word vir smaak* . . . taste. *Ja*, taste! I make it from mango, curry . . ."

"Okay your accent isn't quite like that, but it shares a similarity. Even she thought you were a South African," Jeff whispered teasingly into Issi's ear, but she barely acknowledged him.

An uncomfortable sensation made itself known, as though someone had wrapped a lasso around her midriff and was tightening it with every passing moment. Disembodied voices fought to break free from the shattered fragments of her broken brain. She'd understood the woman's foreign words—but how? And then she spotted the easel standing center to the background of the stall. On it, an artwork . . .

A familiarity Issi couldn't put her finger on filled her head and stirred something in her heart. The style, she knew it . . . but like the foreign words spoken by the stallholder, she was not sure how.

She rubbed the scarred skin behind her left ear. The part of her brain devastated in the bomb blast ached, pleading with her to access what she had lost. Instead, nausea roiled in her belly and left her mouth dry and her vision blurred. Issi instinctively reached out and gripped Jeff's shoulder as her world turned.

"Lovely, are you okay?" Jeff stroked a stray lock off her cheek as Sam came to stand beside her.

"You're white as a sheet. Getting another migraine?" Sam rubbed a caring hand on her back.

Issi nodded, then pointed to the artwork. "How much?" was all she could get her stupid mouth to articulate.

Available here:

https://michelledaltonauthor.com/books/forget-me-not/

ROAD TO REDEMPTION

LOST & FOUND - BOOK TWO

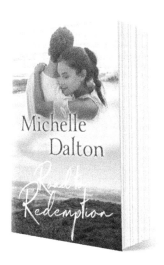

Do second chances count when it's your heart that's on the line?

Raymond sold his soul to protect the only woman he's ever loved. The consequences of his actions leading him down a path of absolute destruction.

Mina vowed she'd never love nor need a man ever again. A self-made business success and single mother, her life is up ended when her past returns.

Dangerous forces are at play and everyone's safety is at stake when poachers threaten all she's worked so hard to achieve, labelling those closest to Mina as suspect.

Will Ray truly be able to take the redemption handed to him and make it work, or will Mina lose her heart and possibly her life to the only man she's ever loved, a second time?

Available here:

https://michelledaltonauthor.com/books/road-to-redemption/

EPONA

THE HIGHLAND SERIES - BOOK ONE

Can love heal all?

A farm attack robs Sadie Munro of her loved ones leaving her scarred and broken. Now her only hope is to escape the country of her birth for a foreign land, far away.

But Sadie's life may still be in danger.

Blane Buchan is an Englishmen seeking a life away from the emptiness of London society and a past he'd rather forget. His heart yearns for a woman who'll love him and not his status or bank account.

Sadie and Blane's paths cross unexpectedly when a mysterious mare appears out of nowhere.

Can Sadie overcome the trauma of her past and find redemption and love in the wild Scottish Highlands?

From the mountains of South Africa to the magical Highland Moors of Scotland, this is a story of redemption, love and the powerful connection between humans and horses.

Available here:

https://michelledaltonauthor.com/books/epona/

VALA

THE HIGHLAND SERIES - BOOK TWO

Is love enough, or will the darkness take over?

Can Calla acknowledge the truth of her past, accept her gift, and embrace an open invitation to love?

On the anniversary of her father's untimely death, forensic anthropologist, Doctor Calla Conroy, is thrown in the deep end of a murder investigation.

To complicate the situation, the voice in her head has returned.

With everything to lose and no time for a psychotic break, Calla ends up in the small highland's village of Lairg. Here she meets the handsome Detective Hamish Bell, who elicits powerful emotions that frighten her.

Can Calla make peace with her traumatic past and the reality of her gift? Or is she simply losing her mind, her heart, and possibly her career?

From the award winning author of *Epona* comes the second in a thrilling women's fiction romance you won't be able to put down.

Available here:

https://michelledaltonauthor.com/books/vala/

Made in the USA
Las Vegas, NV
16 August 2021

28292759R00166